D1413351

MANUFACTURING FOR THE SECURITY OF THE UNITED STATES

Recent Titles from Quorum Books

Expert Systems in Finance and Accounting
Robert J. Thierauf

The Law and Occupational Injury, Disease, and Death
Warren Freedman

Judgment in International Accounting: A Theory of Cognition,
Cultures, Language, and Contracts
Ahmed Belkaoui

The Evolution of Foreign Banking Institutions in the United States:
Developments in International Finance
Faramarz Damanpour

Corporate Planning, Human Behavior, and Computer Simulation:
Forecasting Business Cycles
Roy L. Nersesian

The Valuation and Investment Merits of Diamonds
Sarkis J. Khoury

Market-Oriented Pricing: Strategies for Management
Michael H. Morris and Gene Morris

The Divestiture Option: A Guide for Financial and Corporate
Planning Executives
Richard J. Schmidt

International Perspectives on Trade Promotion and Assistance
S. Tamer Cavusgil and Michael R. Czinkota, editors

The Promise of American Industry: An Alternative Assessment of
Problems and Prospects
Donald L. Losman and Shu-Jan Liang

Global Corporate Intelligence: Opportunities, Technologies, and
Threats in the 1990s
George S. Roukis, Hugh Conway, and Bruce Charnov, editors

The Process of Change in American Banking: Political Economy and
the Public Purpose
Jeremy F. Taylor

Drop Shipping as a Marketing Function: A Handbook of Methods
and Policies
Nicholas T. Scheel

MANUFACTURING FOR THE SECURITY OF THE UNITED STATES

Reviving Competitiveness and Reducing Deficits

Robert E. McGarrah

Q

QUORUM BOOKS

New York • Westport, Connecticut • London

Library of Congress Cataloging-in-Publication Data

McGarrah, Robert E.
Manufacturing for the security of the United States: reviving
competitiveness and reducing deficits / Robert E. McGarrah.
p. cm.
Includes bibliographical references.
ISBN 0-89930-427-3 (lib. bdg. : alk. paper)
1. United States—Manufacturers—Government policy. 2. United
States—Foreign economic relations. 3. Competition, International.
I. Title.
HD9725.M43 1990
338.4'767'0973—dc20   89-28942

British Library Cataloguing in Publication Data is available.

Library of Congress Catalog Card Number: 89-28942
ISBN: 0-89930-427-3

First published in 1990

Quorum Books, 88 Post Road West, Westport, CT 06881
An imprint of Greenwood Publishing Group, Inc.

Printed in the United States of America

The paper used in this book complies with the
Permanent Paper Standard issued by the National
Information Standards Organization (Z39.48-1984).

10 9 8 7 6 5 4 3 2 1

For sons,
Robert and Douglas,
and daughter, Anne Louise

Contents

Introduction

Much more than other institutions, manufacturers of Western Europe, North America, Japan and Asian Rim countries have created ever-increasing expectations for the freedom of common markets and increasing pressure for global interdependence. For different communities, cultures and nations, manufacturers have served as the principal stewards, and their products the principal energizers of dual, industrialized revolutions of societies' rising expectations and rising capabilities derived from heuristic powers of science and technology and increased power for political and economic competitiveness in global market transactions, or geopolitical/military competitiveness in international security affairs. Of course, because those powers are the primary means of human and social progress or of ensuring national security, they have had to be exercised by, and accountable to, the societies and nations they serve. Whether from their contributions to Western powers for military deterrence or to Western powers for political and economic competitiveness, manufacturers of Western nations have exerted a key influence to prompt the recent historical changes occurring in global relationships: between East and West (Communist/Marxist and

Democratic/Capitalist) and between north and south (industrialized and developing/Third World nations).

However, in international markets the competitive standing of U.S. manufacturers has been declining, and among Western democratic, industrial nations the political and economic power of the U.S. government has, consequently, declined. Thus it is virtually impossible to overstate the importance of American manufacturers' management of their own corporate operating competitiveness in the United States and foreign markets, and the importance of the U.S. government's conversion of national security strategies, which, inevitably, American manufacturers will continue to serve. U.S. manufacturers operate at the vortex of challenges: whether American productivity, per capita wealth and living standards will continue to lag or keep pace with those of allied nations, notably Western Europe and Japan; requirements for Western military deterrence, or for joint ventures with Eastern Europe, the Soviets or the Chinese; U.S. trade deficits and financial deficits of about $3.4 trillion; U.S. federal deficits of $3 trillion; stagnating trade and rising gaps of wealth between the United States and Third World nations, notably Latin America, and the $3 trillion of financial deficits those nations have with the United States.

Since World War II—as the results of the Marshall Plan, International Monetary Fund, the World Bank, General Agreement on Tariffs and Trade, and, not least, of foreign operations by American manufacturers—U.S. political and economic freedom has offered the most significant, critical, mass-market opportunities for trade sought by developing nations. In recent years, those opportunities have been cherished and financed increasingly by Western European industrialized nations and Japan. Those freedoms can be preserved, transactions for international interdependence can be expanded and strengthened and U.S. foreign trade deficits can be eliminated, but only if American manufacturers improve their competitiveness. Rules of international manufacturers' market performance and financial accountability need to be made more uniform, equitable and, of course, upheld or enforced. Unfortunately, efforts to reduce requirements for corporate competitiveness exerted in the name of national political and economic security or sovereignty, or nationalistic protectionism, are probably foredoomed (just as the East-West arms race and cold war are being transformed) by the force of global industrial revolutions of rising expectations. American political and economic freedom must be sustained by American manufacturers' capabilities to produce better quality, more easily obtainable, lower priced products for more American and foreign customers.

The decline and revival of U.S. manufacturers are vital requirements for peaceful, equitable international relations, and thus for U.S. national security. Therefore, the U.S. government and manufacturers must change their policies so that like the Japanese, whose competitiveness has grown to challenge American security, they can work together more effectively to fulfill those requirements.

This is not to suggest that the U.S. government adopt a national security policy that would be formulated and conducted by an American bureaucratic counterpart of Japan's Ministry of International Trade and Industry (MITI). American manufacturers do not need to be told what technology they must develop. It is best for American manufacturers to decide for themselves on behalf of their own corporate stakeholders and in keeping with principles of free democratic, competitive market responsibilities, risks and rewards of industrial security and competitiveness. Rather, it is to suggest that, compared with their more competitive Japanese counterparts, American manufacturers need more democratic, participatory management flexibility and much less bureaucratic, technocratic and hierarchical rigidity and delay in deciding and executing quality and productivity improvements. American manufacturers need flexible production, product-quality innovations and must choose their own technology for their products and processes. And thus, together with their customers, they need *simultaneously to build economies of scale and economies of change* that are best suited for their customers' rising expectations and their own rising capabilities.

The federal government's needs are for policy changes in the Pentagon's management of conventional arms procurement and export. Instead of redundant funds and industrial capabilities for different weapons procured for the same military missions and instead of competing for export sales of those weapons to nonaligned governments, the United States would cooperate with the governments of NATO, Japan and Australia to fund programs for sharing the military/industrial burden, for cost reduction and for strengthening their bonds of interdependence. Thus they would provide the opportunity for their defense contractors to compete, consort together or to merge corporate capabilities. A common Western defense market could develop and produce standard conventional weapons needed for Western democracies to face new challenges and security requirements for military deterrence of the 1990s and the twenty-first century.

Western governments' military/industrial cooperation would provide income, employment and export opportunities for their industries. These opportunities would also provide incentives for allied, partner governments to boost their per capita defense expenditures so that the U.S. government could safely reduce its per capita expenditures for defense, and Western military/industrial burdens would thus be shared equally, while total burdens would be reduced because of lower costs of operating, supplying, maintaining and training military personnel for standard weapons. For the U.S. government, this would mean a reduction in annual Pentagon expenditures and the federal deficit of about $100 billion. And the common Western defense market created by U.S.-allied cooperative weapons acquisition programs would strengthen U.S. leadership and the bonds of Western interdependence; it would also divert and reduce nationalistic, political pressure for industrial/economic protectionism that have been exacerbated by the U.S. federal deficits, trade deficits and by inequities of sharing the burden of defense by the Western democratic allies.

In effect, Washington's initiatives for sharing the Western military/industrial burden would be the first stage of the federal government's process for supporting the revival of U.S. manufacturers' competitiveness and for converting U.S. national security strategies to those for civil/industrial progress and interdependence in domestic and foreign affairs.

The next stages would involve reinvestments of the federal savings from sharing the Western defense burden and savings likely to accrue as the result of arms-reduction agreements with the Soviets. Federal deficits and the excessive political and economic burden from dependence on foreign capital, which those deficits required, could be reduced. A civil/industrial university complex for research and development of technology could be established for product innovations and productivity improvements by U.S. manufacturers, and operations of that complex could be conducted on the basis or precedents established by the U.S. government, university and industrial complex for agricultural interdependence, product innovations, productivity and global competitiveness by American enterprise. It would be necessary to repair and improve U.S. public infrastructure systems as well as educational and health delivery facilities; highway, rail, air, and space transportation; and water resources and land conservation. Solid and nuclear waste treatment have been neglected far too long; they are needed for U.S. weapons manufacturers to sustain their employment and convert their operations to meet domestic security needs of American communities, regions and states. State and local governments would join with the federal government in funding infrastructure improvements for developing industry, providing jobs, and reducing the costs of poverty, crime and alienation as well as reducing drug traffic caused by years of neglect and disintegration of the American network of public infrastructure systems and facilities. Cooperative efforts by Western democracies and nonaligned nations should be initiated for a sort of Marshall Plan revival so that U.S. manufacturers could be afforded new and significant opportunities to develop export markets and reduce U.S. trade deficits. At the same time, nonaligned countries could be afforded employment, income and export trade opportunities, not only to reduce their financial deficits with Western nations, but to reduce the gaps of political and economic freedom and standard of living that have widened and threatened the security of both Western democracies and developing nations in a world that no longer needs to be preoccupied with security and power for military deterrence, armed insurgency, repression or terrorists.

It seems appropriate to conclude this prologue with a note on the historical cycle of interdependence managed by the U.S. government and U.S. manufacturers. It was not until President

Franklin Roosevelt dedicated American manufacturers to serve
as the arsenal of democracy in 1940, that they began their revival
from the Great Depression of the 1930s. Their exemplary management of production during and after World War II not only
saved Western democracies from fascism, but made it possible
for democratic governments and manufacturers of West Germany and Japan to recover quickly from their complete devas-
tation, and within 20 years grow to become world-class, political,
economic and financial powers and top competitors in global
markets for consumer/industrial products. And since 1965, the
U.S. government has suffered the loss of political and economic
power while U.S. manufacturers suffered the loss of their competitive power in the global market for consumer/industrial
products. They ignored President Dwight Eisenhower's warning
in 1958 of dangers from the U.S. military/industrial complex. For
the sake of security via strategies for global military deterrence,
they persisted with growth of the U.S. arsenal of democracy into
a global industrial hegemony and domestic industrial pork barrel. Even though U.S. manufacturers developed and applied
high technology for military products and processes of the U.S.
arsenal, they lost their competitive advantage for exploiting that
high technology in global markets for consumer/industrial products. As Japanese and West German manufacturers demonstrated with steel products and automobiles from "low-tech,"
"smokestack" industries and VCRs, television sets and microelectronic chips from "high-tech," "electronic artificial intelligence" industries, those competitive strengths must be derived
from the open democratic and free-market disciplines of industrial performance accountability that are not possible from experiences of arsenals or arms/industrial hegemonies.

Thus U.S. manufacturers' revival in the 1990s and twenty-first
century is linked with the U.S. government's conversion to the
dual strategies and requirements of the security of Western democracies: military/industrial and civil/industrial growth and interdependence.

Manufacturers: Prime Generators of Industrial Progress

The major premise of this book is that manufacturing firms are pivotal institutions for the progress and power of industrial civilization. Although widely accepted and enacted throughout U.S. history, paradoxically this premise now requires advocation in order to preserve our industrial leadership as Americans commence the third century of self-governance. During recent decades, leaders of U.S. industry and government have either denied its validity or accepted it as a truism to be ignored in managing domestic and international security affairs. The U.S. share of world trade of manufactured goods declined from 25 percent in 1953 to 8 percent in 1986.[1] And this evidence is well known. But evidence of the importance of consensus about causes of the decline and commitments to revive American-based manufacturing has not grown so apparent. Examples include the "rustbelt" of "smokestack" industries of the midwestern states; the rising U.S. trade and federal deficits; declining productivity, product quality and market competitiveness of U.S. manufacturers vis-à-vis their Japanese or West German counterparts; and the increase in poverty and decrease in Americans' purchasing power and standard of living compared with those of Western Europeans, while total U.S. employment increased during 1984–89. Concerns have grown about the decline of American power and industrial progress but not about the decline in the role of American manufacturing firms in U.S. foreign and domestic security affairs.

In this chapter, I hope to convince the reader that manufacturing firms are vital institutions requiring the top-priority attention of U.S. industrial and governmental leaders: first, by examining myths of accounting for economic and social progress; second, by comparing manufacturing firms with other institutions from the standpoint of their contribution to the growth in freedom and power of interdependence; and third, by noting their crucial role in preserving global industrial peace and security.

MYTHS OF ACCOUNTING FOR INDUSTRIAL PROGRESS

Historians and economists have accounted for industrial progress by measuring evolutionary changes in kinds of institutional employment and income. Accordingly, industrial progress has occurred because of the mass movement of people from farms to factories for their livelihood and then from blue-collar factory jobs to white-collar service industry jobs. Such accounting is the source of ironies from prevailing myths about the role of manufacturing firms. As more jobs and income are provided by U.S. service industries, U.S. leaders have been executing a deliberate decline in socioeconomic power and industrial progress by U.S. manufacturing industries. This decline is widely accepted as an inevitable consequence of society's progress toward "industrial maturity."

But such accounting ignores the importance of manufacturers as the necessary impetus for growth in employment and income of service institutions. Of all industrial societies' institutions, manufacturing firms uniquely execute the changes in the relationships between human, material and energy information that cause proliferation and changes by all other institutions. Governmental, research, educational, health, cultural or financial institutions and agricultural, mining, transportation or other service industries may be originators of knowledge and providers of resources required by manufacturers. But whether to stimulate or to respond to the need for power or progress by others, manufacturers are the only institutions that combine and execute transformations of those resources into processes and products affecting changes by all institutions of society.

Because of productivity growth and product innovations by manufacturers, the predominant institution for American agricultural employment was transformed from the family farm into today's agribusiness university complex. In 1850, about 64 percent of American workers were employed on farms; in 1929, 20 percent, and in 1984, 3 percent were employed.[2] The Morrill Act of Congress in 1863 established public land-grant colleges of agricultural mechanical arts to educate farmers and agricultural agents of government. However, by using steam energy, electricity and then internal combustion engines as well as knowledge gained from land-grant colleges, manufacturers produced the agrichemicals and equipment for planting, cultivating, harvesting, processing and transportation that enabled farms to exploit that knowledge. Thus manufacturers have not only been pivotal causes of the decline in farm employment and growth in farm productivity, but also of the growth of agricultural and environmental research services, food processing industries and agricultural exports. Today, these industries are strong contributors to improved living standards and political and economic security for all Americans.

Similarly, U.S. manufacturers of automotive, aircraft, electronic computers, machine tools, pharmaceuticals and audiovisual communications equipment were pivotal institutions for growth of domestic and international markets for their own products. They also had a significant impact on spawning and facilitating growth in public and private employment and income of service industries for construction, transportation, audiovisual and print information, supply, maintenance, health, education, and finance.

Because manufacturers have uniquely been producers or executors of changes in human, material and energy information systems that facilitate progress or power, it follows that productivity growth and product innovations by manufacturers are vital determinants of security and progress of each nation, whether classified as a new, industrializing country or as a mature, industrialized society. The importance of manufacturing firms does not decline because of shifts in preponderant employment from farms to factories and then to service industries. Industrial progress always depends on manufacturers' innovations, which serve not only to stimulate or respond to society's needs and expectations, but also to expand opportunities for all other institutional contributions to social progress.

Thus it should be clear that Japanese manufacturers have been the major impetus for expanding not just their own marketing power but the political, economic and monetary power of the Japanese government and Japanese financial institutions (vis-à-vis their American or European counterpart institutions) to influence international political, industrial, economic and monetary affairs. As of December, 1987, the world's top 10 banks, ranked according to the dollar value of their deposits, were all Japanese banks.[3] Not one of the top 25 banks was a U.S. bank. Consider these statistics in light of the 1975–85 growth in U.S. trade deficits with Japan and the decline of U.S. manufacturers' competitive standing with Japanese counterparts. Do they not suggest that growth or decline of financial institutions depend more than ever on growth or decline of manufacturing institutions?

Deceptions from accounting for socioeconomic progress are insidious and powerful. Yet, they are understandable and avoidable, if we keep in mind differences between *accounting* for indications of *results* of *socioeconomic progress* and *managing changes* in *industrial resources, processes* and *products* necessary for socioeconomic progress to occur. Consider an analogy: How we score results of competitive games of sport cannot be the sole determinant of how competitive games have been or should be played in order to set new records; and how we account for or measure results of institutional or socioeconomic progress should not be considered the most valid or reliable indicator of how industrial progress can be sustained in competitive markets or international security affairs.

Socioeconomic financial-accounting data are empirical indi-

cators of the progress achieved in the past. But they are not
always reliable determinants of how progress will be achieved
in the future, because changes are necessary. Moreover, money,
time and social statistics are common denominators for measuring and comparing changes in *economic* status, but not *industrial* status of a society or its institutions. Changes or comparisons
of industrial status are indicated by measuring quality characteristics and the availability (i.e., quantity, time and geographic
location) of products or processes. Quality characteristics refer
to technical specifications of physical or chemical properties.
These specifications are made by designers and developers of
products and processes. Quality specifications also refer to aes-
thetic and/or utilitarian properties specified by users of products
and processes. Availability specifications are also with reference
to consumers or users of products or processes. There are no
common denominators of industrial value or status. Myriad dimensions of quality and availability of products or processes
cannot be reduced to a few common dimensions that are counterparts of those of money, time and people, which define economic status.

Economic measures (e.g., wealth, profitability and population) and industrial measures (e.g., power, productivity and
efficiency) are presumed to be correlated. Both kinds of measure
indicate the status of growth of human social enterprise. They
are also mutually dependent. But, as suggested by the recent
measures of Japan and the United States, economic progress is
more dependent on manufacturing/industrial progress than vice
versa. Economic progress is affected by changes in society's
transaction agreements on supply, demand and price of *existing
qualities* of goods and services. But, in addition to supply, demand and price, manufacturers are the principal institutions of
changing the *qualities* of goods and services exchanged.

Within manufacturing organizations, managers concerned
primarily with qualities and time/rates of the flow of materials
and products are called operations managers. They have attitudes and concerns that differ from financial managers, who
concentrate primarily on cash flow and measures of profitability.
Since World War II, and in the United States more than in foreign
manufacturing firms, computerized electronic-accounting sys-

tems have provided financial (or economic) measurements, summaries and disseminations of expenses, costs and income. Consequently, financial managers of U.S. manufacturing firms have provided faster and more accurate information to top executives and have assumed a greater power than operations managers. Their presumptions that economic or financial progress and industrial progress are mutually dependent or that profitability is more important than productivity have become ironies from financial myths of accounting industrial progress.

In his book *The Reckoning*, David Halberstam described the conflicts between financial managers (or "bean counters") and operations managers (or "car men") of the Ford Motor Company.[4] While bean counters prevailed, the company developed and marketed the Edsel, which proved to be a competitive failure and demonstrated that car men are best able to match technical and logistical capabilities of product and process with qualities the user, or customer, desires or needs. Furthermore, those who plan, measure and control cash flow for economic or financial progress tend to defeat their own purposes, because they tend to usurp the power and responsibility from those concerned with the realities of industrial progress, productivity and market competitiveness.

Historically, financial organizations of corporations have exerted priority uses of computer information systems for performance accounting and management in terms of money and time dimensions. Of course, information per se is a vital source of power, and profit is the universally acclaimed measure of bottom-line performance by industrial processes. With faster, more accurate computerized information, financial managers have exerted a greater influence with top executives of U.S. manufacturing firms. And, like historians and economists, top manufacturing executives have tended to deceive themselves. They have acted as if industrial progress and market competitiveness are managed (i.e., planned and controlled) according to performance measured by financial or cost accountants. Accordingly, U.S. manufacturers have executed strategies for corporate growth via financial conglomeration and divestures, and diverted financial resources needed to sustain corporate security and growth via productivity, product innovations and market competitiveness. In effect, they have deliberately executed a decline in American capabilities for industrial progress, because they concentrate more on economic progress and less on industrial progress.

Thus I trust this discussion has been adequate to raise concerns about the importance of manufacturers as institutions for industrial progress: Industrial progress is an essential prerequisite of economic progress, and economic and financial accounting conventions and performance measurements tend to be deceptive indicators of industrial and economic progress. Industrial progress is indicated by changes in qualities or products and processes (i.e., human, material and energy information systems), in other words, changes in "real wealth" or power. Economic progress is measured in terms of money and time, or "paper wealth."

THE POWERS OF INTERDEPENDENCE

Manufacturers are the most important industrial institution, because changes in their processes and products enable the expansion of the powers of human or social interdependence. By this I mean that innovations of manufacturers' products or processes cause affairs of society to grow more freely specialized *and* more tightly organized to ensure industrial/economic progress.

Industrial progress stems from discoveries and exploitations of universal laws of science, which have sustained dual social revolutions: people's rising expectations of freedoms, powers or responsibilities, together with the revolution of rising capabilities of institutions, which stimulate and respond to peoples' expectations. Manufacturers are especially important because they operate at the confluence of these dual revolutionary forces for industrial progress.

Since their inception as institutions about 300 years ago, manufacturers have combined applications of laws of natural science with applications of human and social laws of politics, economics and morality. Their processes and products facilitate research and development of new scientific laws and, consequently, of new processes and products. Thus by changing human, material and energy information systems, which define their processes and products, manufacturers execute key roles in converting the heuristic power of science and technology into a more highly specialized and organized social force for industrial progress. In other words, manufacturers create more freedom for more specialized interests, and they expand society's responsibility and power of interdependence. Consider some examples.

From 1983 to 1986, the dollar value of electronics in the average car manufactured in North America increased from about $425 to $825. Manufacturers designed and produced new engines equipped with computers to reduce fuel consumption, to improve engine performance and to facilitate the diagnoses of engine problems to improve engine maintenance. Not only have the computers worked as intended, they have also changed the skill requirements of auto maintenance mechanics. General Motors, Ford and Chrysler have established auto maintenance training programs at community colleges throughout the United States.[5] Auto manufacturers and educational institutions are more interdependent, and auto engine maintenance has become the work of electronic mechanical technicians, not the greasy job for high-school dropouts.

This is but one, small illustration of the growth in the power of synergism and interdependence among manufacturers of microelectronic circuits, computers, automobiles and service institutions for maintenance, education and finance. Synergism of a much greater scope has resulted from the growth in interdependence of practically all American institutions (public or private, profit making or nonprofit) affected by high-tech manufacturers of microelectronic circuits, computers and audiovisual communications equipment. These manufacturers have created and expanded new institutions and caused older, established manufacturing and service institutions to grow more interdependent by their use of common information facilities, equipment and networks.

The acronym CAD-CAM (computer assisted design-computer assisted manufacture) describes the practicalities and necessities for growth in interdependence among organizational functions (technical, financial, legal and operational) involved in product design, process design and process controls by firms of smoke-stack industries (foundries, electric power utility installations, smelters, steel mills and machine tool and automobile factories) and by high-tech firms. CAD-CAMs are human, material and energy information systems for "flexible manufacturing" so that changes in product qualities and process capabilities are made much more rapidly, much less expensively and with greater ensurance of providing for improvements needed or desired by society.

Thus more than other industrial institutions, manufacturers have provided not just employment for expanding the variety of engineering, economic, legal or functional specialists, but common information and equipment enabling those specialists to coordinate their work more efficiently. In effect, manufacturers have expanded and strengthened the bonds of interdependence within and among institutions of society as well as among nations.

Former equipment operators, shop superintendents, functional managers and corporate executives of steel companies now increasingly depend on computerized information to effectively combine their jobs of producing larger quantities and better qualities of specialty steel products. Traditional distinctions between hierarchies and bureaucracies are becoming blurred, not just because factory workers and office workers perform white-collar jobs, but also because employees of all organizational ranks and functions are working together with greater interdependence facilitated by computerized information.

There may be questions of whether CAD-CAM or other computer systems cause relations among line staff managers and workers to become more rigid, technocratic and less flexible, or more democratic, humanistic and enjoyable (not to say, productive, too). The answer to such questions depends on managers' and employees' sharing of costs, risks and benefits from acquiring, adapting and operating CAD-CAM systems to suit the needs of their product, processes and customers. Without mutual involvement by all stakeholders (designers, installers, operators, maintainers and users), computer information systems are bound to fail. But there is no question that computer information systems not only facilitate but require greater interdependence among all levels and functions of their corporate stakeholders or that their greater independence and more effective cooperation are required for product and process innovations to cause growth in corporate productivity, profitability or competitiveness.

INTERNATIONAL INTERDEPENDENCE

Since World War II, the growth of human and organizational interdependence generated by manufacturing firms has extended well beyond geopolitical boundaries. International interdependence among industrial institutions has generated forces for unprecedented, political and economic interdependence among national governments. Manufacturers' product and process innovations have been pivotal forces for the growth in the bonds of interdependence among people, institutions and nations.

It is true that U.S. government policies and political and economic programs such as the Marshall Plan, General Agreement on Tariffs and Trade, International Monetary Fund and United Nations Programs (e.g., Food and Agricultural Organization and United Nations Industrial Development Organization) provided principles and policies fostering international interdependence. However, more concretely, the technical and industrial expansion of manufacturers' products and processes to the international scale of operations has made international interdependence a practical way of life, even a requirement for industrial/economic survival.

Not long ago, the strongest political force for U.S. political and economic isolation emanated from the Western states with the largest farm employment. However, U.S. farmers have more recently become strong political advocates of expanded international trade with the Soviet Union, largely because of their experience with the growth and expansion of the markets by the U.S. agriindustrial complex, fostered mainly by manufacturers.

In 1988, 12 European governments resolved that their nations would become a common market in 1992. American, Canadian and Japanese as well as European manufacturers have expanded their operations in Europe since the end of World War II, when Jean Monnet proclaimed his visions of the European Common Market. This resolution by European government leaders was a consequence of European industrial progress. Manufacturers' exploitations of universal laws of science had grown to require more uniformity and consistency among sovereign nations' laws affecting industrial and economic growth. Without common, international laws and markets for industrial accountability, manufacturers cannot freely continue to improve products and processes for industrial growth and international interdependence.

Also in 1988, the United States and Canada negotiated terms for a common North American market. And Washington enacted legislation (1) to encourage more equitable (common) market conditions for the industrializing countries of South Korea, Taiwan, Singapore, Hong Kong and Brazil and (2) to authorize retaliatory or protectionist measures against those nations whose governments refuse free access for U.S. industries to operate in their national markets. Thus U.S. government leaders have acted to reinforce the pressure for common international laws of political and economic and industrial accountability and greater interdependence of the United States with other sovereign nations. This pressure emanated chiefly from manufacturing firms controlled by foreign and by American stakeholders.

As they have internationalized their operations, manufacturers have had, pragmatically, to confront, accommodate or ameliorate *cultural* differences including language, customs, attitudes, social values, etc. Different societies accept, resist and adjust in different ways to manufacturers' products and processes, because, instinctively perhaps, they tend to preserve their identity even while they join the industrial revolution of peoples' rising expectations and manufacturers' rising capabilities. Thus manufacturers have changed their human, material and energy information systems to accommodate cultural differences. And societies have changed their cultural distinctions to gain advantages from manufacturers' development and application of the natural laws of science and technology.

As manufacturers manage to expand and strengthen industrial/economic bonds of international interdependence more rapidly, controversies will grow about whether social or cultural differences prevail or are subsumed by processes of industrial-ization. But these controversies are probably more academic and esoteric than practical, because all societies and cultures have enlisted in the industrial revolution and because manufacturers have pragmatically demonstrated their effectiveness in dealing with cultural differences. Consider some examples.

During the 1960s, the French expressed apprehension about Americans' "Coca-Cola-nization" of their culture. However, while Coca-Cola markets in France have grown, French wine markets in the United States have grown perhaps even more dramatically. And French-American concordance and contro-versy remain lively, yet as peaceful as ever.

Cultural differences are often cited to explain why Japanese financial and manufacturing firms have gained, while their American counterparts have lost competitive standing in world markets. For example, Americans have concluded that Japanese companies have grown more productive because Japanese cul-ture stresses response and conformance with group values or norms, whereas American cultural values emphasize the expres-sion of individual human freedom. But Japanese authorities have stated that their manufacturers have grown more competitive because they have applied the concepts and techniques for man-aging product and process quality that they learned during the postwar years from the American consultant W. Edwards Dem-ing. Meanwhile, international markets continue to grow and bonds of Japanese-American interdependence are strengthened, because Japanese and American manufacturers and financial in-stitutions act more often and pragmatically, case by case, to compete, consort together in joint ventures or merge interests in product and process innovations and economic growth.

The expansion of common international markets by the indus-tries of Western European, North American and East Asian countries has had unacknowledged effects on the Soviet and Chinese communist nations. For such expansion is clear evi-dence of the greater power of Western political and economic ideology in managing global industrial revolutions of peoples' rising expectations and institutions' (mainly manufacturers') ris-ing capabilities to stimulate and respond to those expectations.

Recently, Soviet and Chinese Marxist leaders have had pragmatically and carefully to adopt their (limited) versions of Western democratic competitive policies for their agricultural, manufacturing and service industries to serve people's needs and desires for progress as well as to preserve their security in governing affairs of Marxist nations in relation with Western nations. In effect, concerns for political and economic security have been growing among Marxist and capitalist nations, because of growing pressures for international interdependence and changes in sovereign powers of national governments.

These changes are the result of strategies for industrial growth primarily executed by manufacturers, whose products and markets facilitated the growth of agricultural and service industries. Companies in those industries have acted freely, competitively and more rapidly to develop and apply laws of science and technology across international boundaries. Thus while industries have created common international markets and strengthened international bonds of industrial/economic interdependence, they have also expanded and strengthened the international requirements for more uniform and equitable terms of accountability and performance by multinational industrial firms. And these requirements are practically universal (i.e., technical, financial, legal, social and ecological), because multinational industrial growth is based on the laws of science and technology, which are themselves universal.

CHANGING U.S. STRATEGIES

De facto since World War II, international interdependence and fair, uniform, industrial market, performance and accountability requirements have been U.S. strategies for international peacekeeping and national security. Accordingly, U.S. manufacturers have internationalized their operations for product research, development, production and marketing and U.S. government leaders executed policies and programs such as those of the Marshall Plan, United Nations, General Agreement on Tariffs and Trade, the International Monetary Fund and Overseas Private Investors Corporation. However, during the 1950s and early 1960s, while Japanese and Western Europeans rebuilt their industries and emulated or improved policies and practices of U.S. manufacturers, major American firms neglected their obligation to their customers of quality assurance, or minimum defects, and granted annual automatic wage increases based on the historical U.S. productivity growth rate during 1902–50 of 3.3%. And companies such as ITT and Textron converted their growth strategies from corporate operational competitiveness to corporate financial conglomeration. American customers and industrial leaders ignored the trends of growth in imports from firms such as Sony, Volkswagen and Toyota, and since the early 1970s, American manufacturing competitiveness has been below that of its foreign counterparts. This has caused unprecedented growth of U.S. deficits in international trade and in international public and private financial transactions. While Americans increased the political pressure for protection against exports by foreign manufacturers and Washington leaders adjusted U.S. dollar supplies, interest rates and foreign currency exchange rates, foreign governments and manufacturers managed to sustain their production and growth in exports to the vast, critical-mass, U.S. market. Yet, it has been the decline in U.S. manufacturers' performance (i.e., productivity or market competitiveness) that has forced escalated exports of foreign capital to finance U.S. federal deficits and private expenditures—and has strained the bonds of U.S. leadership and international interdependence among Western and developing nations.

The rise in competitive standing of West German and Japanese manufacturers and decline of American manufacturers signifies the changing requirements and priorities for U.S. security. Put simply, U.S. manufacturers have not been capable of responding to the growth in the need for all the "guns and butter" required to sustain Americans' expectations, leadership and security of Western (free-world) affairs, and Americans cannot afford to sustain the growth in their trade and financial deficits to Western allied nations much longer. In other words, U.S. manufacturers are needed more to restore and sustain U.S. security in political and economic industrial affairs of international markets for civil/industrial products and services, and U.S. security policies should be changed to reduce safely U.S. manufacturers' responsibility and role in geopolitical/military affairs of U.S. and Western security.

Possible changes in security policies will be examined in later discussions. The point for emphasis in this discussion is the importance of strong, competitive manufacturing firms as the vital, pivotal institutions of national and international security affairs, civil as well as military.

LIMITS TO INDUSTRIAL GROWTH

This brings us to a final concern about the importance of manufacturing firms. As primary executors of processes for industrial and economic growth, manufacturers have the greatest stake in managing those processes so that their limits are never exceeded and the decline or collapse of industrial civilization is averted.

Exponential growth of industrial powers or economic wealth is the ethic of survival of industrial civilization. Institutions must be managed so that they grow at exponential rates, or else they decline and "die."

In 1972 the Club of Rome published *Limits to Growth*, a global study of processes for growth of industrial/economic wealth and population, by computer systems experts of M.I.T.[6] Their conclusions were that growth processes were unmanageable and foredoomed to collapse, because they would exceed the limits of (1) the earth's nonrenewable resources, (2) toleration by nature's ecological, life-support systems to survive while sustaining growth in pollution and (3) moral toleration by societies' political and economic systems of widening gaps of the wealth and power wrought by the growth processes. *Limits to Growth* provoked widespread controversy about the validity or realities of the limits and about the effectiveness of the regulators of growth. Issues were about whether free-market economic forces of supply, demand and price, together with governmental laws and educational (scientific, technological) developments, would effectively sustain exponential growth rates without exceeding their limits. To emphasize their conclusion, M.I.T. researchers cited the analogy of lilies growing at the rate of 50 percent each day in a lily pond with an area big enough for 30 days' growth and asked, "When is the lily pond half-full?" The answer, of course, is the 29th day—almost certainly too late for industrial democracies to take action to ensure sustaining processes for exponential growth.

Critics of *Limits to Growth* found errors in the computer programs, which discredited the validity of the results of the M.I.T. study process and diverted attention from the controversies. Yet, today, manufacturers' growth management is the recognized means to resolve the two most profound security requirements of global civilization: (1) to avoid the collapse of nature's life-support systems and (2) to avoid holocaust from intended or accidental use of nuclear weapons. These requirements are for manufacturing firms to change their human, material and energy information systems to sustain industrial progress and processes for industrial and economic growth.

Exhaust gases of coal, oil or gasoline fuels and wastes of nuclear fuels for energy are causing not only toxic damage to humans and the natural environment, but also the erosion of the earth's ozone protection from solar heat and the greenhouse effect of rising temperature. Also, the number and power of nuclear weapons have grown beyond their effective use as a means for exercising political power to ensure national and international peace and security. Thus management of manufacturers' products and processes is a moral concern of global survival. If industrial/economic progress is to be sustained and human ecology systems are to survive then, somehow, manufacturing firms must exert pivotal roles in stimulating and responding to security requirements for industrial civilizations.

SUMMARY

Manufacturers' products and processes are comprehensive human, material and energy information systems that change purposes and processes of other institutions (agricultural, mining, services, information, financial, educational, and governmental) more than vice versa.

The importance of manufacturing firms has been ignored because of the confusing myths of accounting for *economic* progress with management of *industrial* progress. Quantitative results of industrial change are indicated by economic, financial or cost-accounting data and accepted conventions about their compilation and uses. But scientific and engineering data are prerequisites for managing causes and qualitative and quantitative effects of industrial change, and manufacturers are the principal institutions or executors of industrial change. The preponderant institutions for Americans' employment and income shifted historically from farms to factories. But this shift occurred because of industrial progress by manufacturers. More recently, and dramatically, Americans' main source of employment and income shifted from manufacturing to the service industries. This shift is ominous. American per capita hourly income and standard of living have declined. And the shift to service industries occurred more because of the decline in productivity, competitiveness and exports by American-based manufacturers (both low-technology smokestack firms and high-tech firms, vis-à-vis their foreign counterparts) than because of evolutionary proliferation and growth of U.S. service industries. Indeed, U.S. service industries have grown more dependent on foreign manufacturers, and this has made it more urgent for American manufacturers to restore their competitive standing.

Manufacturers have been the pivotal institutions for globalizing industrial revolution, i.e., for proliferation and growth in the power of specialized production and distribution capabilities and growth in the requirement for peaceful interdependence among demanders and providers of those capabilities. Evidence is clear from the growth in importance of more common industrial rules for market competition and corporate accountability. Common international markets for manufactured products have been significantly expanded among countries of North America, Western Europe and the so-called Asian Rim countries of Japan, South Korea, Taiwan, Hong Kong, Australia, and Singapore. Political and economic accommodations, cooperation and stronger bonds on interdependence are required among sovereign governments of nations with long histories as former wartime enemies. These trends have prompted the Soviet and Chinese governments to modify their Marxist communist doctrines and adopt more democratic free-market principles for managing industrial growth.

If global exponential growth of industrial power, economic wealth and population is to be sustained, then manufacturers' products and processes must soon be changed to avert their collapse, before limits of human toleration of armed violence or nuclear holocaust are surpassed or limits of nature's toleration of industrial pollution are exceeded.

Manufacturers have developed and produced unprecedented quantities of more lethal weapons. Nuclear weapons have been produced and deployed, mostly by the United States and Soviet superpowers, according to their security strategies for mutual deterrence from military attack. But manufacturers of other nations have developed and produced nuclear weapons to enhance the geopolitical security of their governments, for example, the United Kingdom, France, China, Israel, South Africa and India. Meanwhile, manufacturers in a growing number of nations have substantially increased the lethality and availability of so-called conventional (i.e., nonnuclear) weapons. During recent years, conventional weapons have been used increasingly by terrorist forces of governments, insurrectionist organizations and international drug purveyors against innocent private citizens involved in the affairs of international interdependence. Thus manufacturers are institutions for increasing, decreasing or controlling conflicts of industrial processes for growth: productive power for more peaceful interdependence versus growth in the power for violent destruction of efforts and bonds of social, economic and international interdependence as well as for nuclear holocaust. Conventional wisdom is that arms control or disarmament are issues for governments to resolve. But governments are national institutions and manufacturers have become international institutions. If they are to remain free self-governing institutions providing industrial and economic progress in all nations, then manufacturers should exert an influential role to reduce the production and distribution of nuclear and conventional weapons.

Manufacturers' products and growth processes emit wastes or pollutants likely to surpass the capabilities of nature's life-support systems. Thus manufacturing firms are important because of their vital role in avoiding global calamity from the greenhouse effect, caused by exhaust from industrial and automotive energy systems, and increases in industrial toxic waste, which diminishes the supplies of potable water required to sustain the exponential rate of global population growth.

In their book *Manufacturing Matters: The Myth of the Post-Industrial Economy*, Professors Stephen Cohen and John Zysman emphasize the importance of manufacturing firms to the security and growth of American economic capabilities, public and private.[7] To this I would add that manufacturing firms are pivotal institutions for the security of all other institutions of industrial civilization. The political, military, environmental, economic and social security of nations depend on industrial progress or competitive standing of their manufacturing firms. Even though they may not be the originators or designated executors of social policies, manufacturers provide the substantive means for those policies to become effective.

My purpose in emphasizing the importance of manufacturing firms has been to encourage more serious consideration of the causes and remedies for the decline of U.S. manufacturers, which is the theme of this book. The aim is not to arouse U.S. political and industrial leaders to try to restore the U.S. industrial/economic hegemony that existed immediately after World War II. This is neither practical nor desirable. Instead, the aim is to convince readers of the importance of restoring U.S. manufacturers' productivity and competitiveness so that U.S. trade and financial deficits are soon eliminated, bonds of international trust and peaceful interdependence can be strengthened and expanded, and processes for industrial growth can be managed to improve the American standard of living and to avoid their inevitable collapse, if their human or ecological limits are exceeded.

NOTES

1. Center for Popular Economics, *Economic Report of the People* (Boston: South End Press, 1986), 33; Kenichi Ohmae, "Don't Blame It on Tokyo," *New Perspectives Quarterly* (Fall 1987): 36.

2. *The New York Times*, July 20, 1988, p. A12, from the U.S. Bureau of the Census.

3. *The New York Times*, July 26, 1988, p. D1, data compiled by the *American Banker*.

4. David Halberstam, *The Reckoning* (New York: Morrow, 1986).

5. Joseph B. White, "Auto Mechanics Struggle to Cope with Technology in Today's Cars," *The Wall Street Journal*, July 26, 1988, p. 37.

6. D. and A. Meadows, *Limits to Growth* (New York: Universe Books, 1972).

7. Stephen S. Cohen and John Zysman, *Manufacturing Matters: The Myth of the Post-Industrial Economy* (New York: Basic Books, 1987).

2

U.S. Manufacturers' Decline: Internal Causes

Having emphasized the importance of manufacturing firms as the pivotal institutions for safeguarding the security and providing power and progress for both industrialized and developing societies, it follows that causes of the decline of U.S. manufacturing should be high-priority concerns of all Americans. Those causes are numerous and complex. Yet they must be understood as the only logical basis for effective remedies to restore manufacturing competitiveness.

We shall consider internal causes to be those under the primary control of manufacturing firms per se. External causes are primary responsibilities of government leaders and will be discussed in the next chapter. Throughout our discussions of causes and remedies, internal and external, we shall keep in mind that they are all interdependent, because governments (local, regional, state and national) depend vitally on manufacturing firms for their security and vice versa.

There is a variety of causes of lost competitiveness controllable by U.S. manufacturers. Some have been acknowledged; others, ignored. Indeed some manufacturers are known to have invested in remedies which, ironically, exacerbated their decline.

In 1983, Mr. James A. Baker, executive vice president of electronic systems of the General Electric Company (GE), said, "American industry faces three choices in the 1980's: Automate, emigrate, or evaporate!"[1] Such a prescription by an executive of a high-tech manufacturing firm with GE's reputation is a rather clear indication that American managers, not foreign competitors, have caused the decline of U.S. manufacturing industry. Thus a major purpose of this chapter is to encourage introspection by U.S. executives who may have reacted to invalid causes or ignored valid causes of their firm's productivity stagnation or lost competitiveness.

OUTSOURCING AND DIVESTMENTS BY U.S. MANUFACTURERS

Executives have cited facts that foreign-based manufacturers incur much lower labor costs and enjoy the competitive advantages of lower prices or higher profits from their exports to the U.S. market. Accordingly, U.S. executives have closed American factories and opened factories in Asia and Latin America to produce products for export to the U.S. market. Or they have divested from manufacturing and invested in service industries of the United States. According to Robert W. Galvin, chairman and CEO of Motorola, Inc., "manufacturers are concluding that a major increase in offshore operations is the only viable choice remaining and essential to our survival."[2]

It is true that "outsourcing" to factories in Asia or Latin America reduces direct labor costs and, perhaps, difficulties with union-management relations. But direct labor costs are only about 10 percent of the total manufacturing costs. And by outsourcing, indirect labor costs and difficulties in relations with governments are increased: Costs of employment security and other fringe benefits such as health, housing, education and retirement tend to be higher in developing countries. Moreover, greater distances from factory sources to American customers add significantly to costs of transporting, supplying, maintaining and improving the quality of products, just in time for meeting customers' desires and needs.

Since 1970, Japanese and European manufacturers have "insourced," while American manufacturers have outsourced more factories to produce products for the U.S. market. These counteracting trends have changed manufacturers' competitive standings perhaps most significantly in markets for high-tech electronic products. By 1988, *foreign manufacturers'* shares were overwhelmingly predominant in U.S. market transactions for VCRs, radios and television equipment and their shares were growing rapidly in U.S. markets for personal computers and electronic components (microelectronic chips, circuits, switches and cathode-ray tubes). U.S. manufacturers had lost American customers' loyalty and faced critical disadvantages in the 1990s market for the "next generation" of electronic products (high definition television equipment and digital and superconductive circuits). Even worse, U.S. manufacturers lost shares of the military electronics market. The U.S. Defense Science Board warned that U.S. military forces were required to depend increasingly on foreign electronics manufacturers, because U.S. manufacturers failed to respond to U.S. military requirements for product quality and technical innovations.[3]

Lionel Trains closed its plant in Michigan and moved to a factory in Tijuana, Mexico. Management required just-fired workers to pack the moving vans—and the company ended up with a jumble of mislabeled parts in Tijuana. And 15 to 20 truckloads were delayed by Mexican customs agents for weeks at the border. There isn't, for example, a Spanish name for a vertical milling machine, and if you can't identify the machine, you can't bring the whole truckload into Mexico. Lionel experienced tremendous problems with quality as a result of a poorly trained Mexican work force. The company could deliver only one-third of its orders on time. Its share of the toy train market slipped from 25 percent to 10 percent; its share of the track market slumped from 75 percent to 25 percent. However, Lionel was able to return to its Michigan factory, rehire approximately 80 percent of its former employees, who agreed to a 40 cent an hour pay cut and a reduction of four paid holidays as part of their new compensation package.[4]

General Instrument Corporation's Taiwan subsidiary found itself competing with 11 companies founded in Taiwan by its former employees.[5]

Thus outsourcing exacerbates loss of competitiveness and profits, because of increased costs of employment, problems in relations with different governments and, most important, costs of delivering product quality innovations just in time for American customers' needs and desires. As Mr. Akio Morita, chairman and CEO of Sony Corporation, said, "We are not taking away your manufacturers' business. They are giving it up. If they move out factories and depend on the Far East, that means the hollowing of American industry."[6]

Analogous to outsourcing, to sustain their economic security, American manufacturers have been divesting from manufacturing and investing in service industries of the United States. For example, GE sold its small appliances and television manufacturing businesses and acquired the National Broadcasting Company (NBC) and the Kidder-Peabody financial services company. Overall, U.S. manufacturing has declined from 30 percent to about 21 percent of the U.S. gross national product (GNP).

Like outsourcing, divestment from U.S. manufacturing into the service industries causes a further decline in U.S. industrial competitiveness, or a further decline in pivotal capabilities (industrial, economic, political and military) of the firms and society. Such divestments ignore that governmental and service institutions depend much more on manufacturing firms than vice versa, and that manufacturing firms, alone, execute innovations in the human, material and energy information systems that determine industrial progress, profitability and economic security for all individuals and institutions.

After relying increasingly on their manufacturing firms for nearly 100 years, most Americans must now depend on lower paying, less-productive jobs in service institutions, financing, operating, maintaining or distributing products of foreign manufacturers. Since 1965, productivity, per capita income and the standard of living have increased much more slowly in America than in Japan or West Germany. And the costs of the widening gaps between rich and poor as well as the declining number of middle-class Americans have grown more evident as demonstrated by social alienation, cynicism, drugs, educational dropouts, poverty and crime.

A society's freedom, responsibility, polity and power of self-governance are substantiated by the management of growth in the productivity and product quality innovations by its manufacturers. Americans require the revitalization of, not the abdication or divestments by, U.S. manufacturers.

LACK OF GOVERNMENT SUPPORT OF U.S. MANUFACTURERS' SECURITY

U.S. manufacturers have also blamed the federal government for their loss of competitiveness with foreign manufacturers who export products or insource factory production for the U.S. market. They allege that foreign governments provide stronger political or economic support for their manufacturers' competitive efforts or that Washington's fiscal and monetary policies, budget deficits or high-interest rates have made the costs of U.S. competitive capabilities (capital funds and prices of U.S. products) too high for them to compete with foreign firms.

It is true that foreign governments support the growth of their manufacturing industries but not substantially more than the U.S. government supports or protects the growth of U.S. producers of weapons, agricultural products, steel or high-tech products. Moreover, it is also true that greater U.S. government support or protection would certainly exacerbate American manufacturers' indolence and consequent loss of productivity or competitiveness and foreign market opportunities.

U.S. strengths continued to grow during the 1950s, not only because American industry escaped destruction from World War II, but also because Americans and their government rejected the political, economic and industrial isolation that had caused the Great Depression and led to the rise of fascism and World War II. Instead, Americans fostered growth in international interdependence so that governments would cooperate and industrial firms could compete freely and fairly, according to the common terms of performance accountability. The U.S. government's strategy since World War II has been for all societies to join in the effort to develop and secure benefits from international common markets. Today, as happened after the adoption of the Glass-Steagall Act, protectionist measures, such as tariffs, taxes, licenses and quotas, would almost certainly provoke retaliation by the governments of trading-partner nations. There would be substantial losses, not just of U.S. private investments and markets in foreign countries, but also of foreign investments providing support for American living standards and growth of U.S. markets of vital concern to American manufacturing and service firms.

More political protection or economic support for private industries result in less competitive capabilities of manufacturing firms, more competition between governments and loss of industrial and economic growth opportunities in expanding common markets and bonds of international interdependence.

Although not a strong consensus agreement by executives or economists, it is nonetheless logical that the high U.S. inflation rates and consequently high U.S. interest rates (set by the Federal Reserve Board to reduce and control U.S. inflation rates) experienced during 1975–84, were the effect of a 10-year decline of U.S. manufacturers' productivity more than the cause of U.S. manufacturers' inabilities to raise and invest the capital needed to finance improvements in product qualities or process productivity. Moreover, after the quadrupling of OPEC oil prices in 1973, Japanese and West German manufacturers suffered much more than American manufacturers, who were far less dependent on OPEC imports. Yet inflation rates in Japan and West Germany remained much lower than in the United States, mainly because the rates of productivity growth and product quality innovations were higher than those of the U.S. manufacturing industry.

The U.S. and Japanese governments agreed on temporary restrictions in growth of U.S. imports of Japanese steel, so that U.S. steel producers could sustain and improve their shares in the U.S. market. After several years, American steel firms improved their profits, but at higher costs for U.S. customers. But instead of reinvesting its profits to improve productivity and the quality of its products (i.e., competitive capabilities) the U.S. Steel Corporation, American's largest steel manufacturer, acquired the Marathon Oil Company, changed its name to the USX Corporation, and reduced its steel manufacturing and marketing operations in the U.S. markets. Thus U.S. manufacturers did not respond.

PRODUCT, PROCESS AND EMPLOYMENT
REGULATIONS BY GOVERNMENT

U.S. manufacturers have also complained that their high costs, lost competitiveness and productivity stagnation were the effect of their compliance with U.S. government regulations on human health, product and process safety, environmental protection and employment opportunities for minorities.

Such complaints are valid only in exceptional cases of manufacturers whose cost advantages or competitive market standing are derived from their inflicting on society the risks and consequently higher, remedial costs of human social and environmental health and safety or of employment discrimination. Or in exceptional cases of overzealous, erroneous enforcement by government bureaucrats.

However, all manufacturers require and apply fair rules of competition and democratic processes for changing those rules. They also require freedom, fairness and improved purchasing power and standard of living for their corporate stakeholders— in other words, minimized risks and costs of human, environmental and social health and safety.

Foreign manufacturers have had to comply with regulations to compete effectively in U.S. markets. It is interesting to note that Japanese auto manufacturers redesigned engine combustion chambers and ignition systems to comply with the U.S. government's regulations of exhaust gas hazards and fuel consumption, while U.S. auto manufacturers added catalytic converters and lobbied successfully to regulate their own rate of reduction in *average fuel consumption* by all automobiles they were producing. In effect, U.S. auto manufacturers probably lost and Japanese manufacturers gained competitive standing awarded by American customers, who found it necessary to express their requirements for product-quality improvements via governmental regulations, because U.S. firms failed to respond.

It is to their competitive advantage for manufacturers to initiate (not to resist) product and process-quality innovations that improve the standard of living, i.e., the conditions for human or environmental health and safety.

SHIFTS TO DEFENSE-PRODUCT MANUFACTURING

American manufacturers have abandoned U.S. markets for consumer/industrial products and invested in developing and producing high-tech weapons for the U.S. Department of Defense. These actions enable American manufacturers to acquire advanced technology and use taxpayers' funds, while minimizing shareowners' financial risks. They not only avoid the high costs of scarce American capital, but also acquire the patent rights to the use of technology for civil products. Not least, weapons manufacturers deal in secrecy, for the most part with a single customer, the Pentagon, which defrays most of their marketing costs in U.S. and foreign markets.

Apparently with such purposes in mind, executives of General Motors (GM) acquired Hughes Aircraft Company, and Singer Manufacturing Company divested from 100 years of operation in the world sewing-machine markets, to concentrate almost exclusively on U.S. military products markets. GE had already ranked among the top 10 U.S. weapons contractors, before acquiring RCA's military electronic equipment manufacturing business.

However, there are more positive, economic and industrial multiplier effects on manufacturers, markets and users of civil products, but *negative*, economic and industrial multiplier effects on manufacturers, markets and users of military products. Civil products enable people and their institutions to work and live more productively, with more powerful bonds for peaceful interdependence, trust and open competitive market accountability, with stronger capability or power for growth and progress than is possible from military products. After all, military products expand society's destructive power, which stems from fear, secrecy, suspicion and distrust, and consumer/industrial products expand society's productive power of freedom and trust. American manufacturers have experienced, even though they have not learned since President Franklin Roosevelt dedicated them as the "arsenal of democracy," that military/industrial growth weakens more than strengthens the capability for competition and accountability required for civil/industrial growth.

Shifts from civil to military product manufacturing have occurred probably more often because of Washington's military security or weapons procurement policies than because of initiatives of U.S. manufacturers. So, for purposes of more comprehensive discussion, I have classified such shifts as external, or governmental, causes of U.S. manufacturers' decline (to be examined in chapter 3), while emphasizing in this discussion that manufacturers have been willingly complicit with, but ignorant of their responsibility for this cause of their decline.

This concludes a brief, but, it is hoped, convincing examination of U.S. manufacturers' self-inflicted causes of the decline in productivity, product innovations and competitiveness in the U.S. and world markets. The causes include outsourcing or closing U.S. factories and opening foreign factories to serve U.S. customers; divesting from U.S. manufacturing and investing in U.S. service industries; blaming Washington's fiscal, monetary or regulatory policies and lobbying for special protection or political and economic support; and increasing emphasis on manufacturing and markets for military products while decreasing emphasis on civil (consumer/industrial) product innovations. It is practically impossible to estimate the *extent* of U.S. manufacturers' decline associated uniquely (or even mainly) with these self-inflicted causes. They are all interrelated with other internal and external causes. These are now discussed with the hope that pragmatic case-by-case remedies can be combined to reduce, if not eliminate, the causes so that U.S. manufacturing competitiveness is revived. It should also be noted that, although it is human to blame others or to ignore causes for one's own management failures, U.S. executives are not politicians and cannot be absolved from market disciplines and obligations of professional honesty, accountability and competitive performance by their manufacturing firms.

One kind of ignorance about causes of manufacturers' decline stems from abuses of computerized financial-management information systems. Managers of corporate financial functions have dominated the management of corporate operations. Corporate goals, performance accounting and the management of profitability have been allowed to conflict with, and to subordinate, the corporate goals of productivity, product innovations and maintenance and growth in competitive standing in product markets. Strategies for corporate growth via financial conglomeration and divestitures have overwhelmed strategies for corporate growth via product innovations and expanded production and marketing operations.

Another kind of controllable cause stems from U.S. manufacturers' failure to organize and develop human resources as effectively as their foreign competitors. Bureaucracies and hierarchies fostering special interests have grown to dominate the common institutional concerns of U.S. manufacturing firms. The quality of corporate work life has eroded. The gaps of privilege, authority, recognition and rewards have widened between those who *manage information* (i.e., plan, design, measure and control) and those who *do* the *work* of adding values to material and products of manufacturing firms. Union leaders and corporate executives have overindulged in adversarial relations and have ignored their mutual responsibilities to their common constituents or corporate stakeholders (employees, suppliers, customers, shareholders, citizens and communities).

ABUSES OF COMPUTERIZED MANAGEMENT INFORMATION SYSTEMS

It is well known that Americans have used computer information systems longer and more extensively than Europeans and the Japanese. Equally well known is the fact that American manufacturers have suffered more from losses of customer loyalty, stagnating productivity, employee morale and employment. Notwithstanding these ironic trends, the strong consensus of most Americans is that the future security and political and economic well-being of the United States will depend increasingly on growth in productivity, product innovations and applications of American computers.

From 1940 to 1980, the proportion of the U.S. work force involved in information jobs grew from 24 percent to 48 percent, according to Marc Porat in his nine-volume study titled *The Information Economy.*[7] With so much more computerized information to manage their affairs, why do more Americans perceive widening gaps between promise and performance by U.S. manufacturing firms?

It is suggested that educators and practitioners of manufacturing management have been abusing and overindulging in empirical information that can be computerized and have been ignoring or distorting information that cannot be computerized. Empirical quantitative information processed by computers is too readily accepted as mathematical, hence scientifically valid or rigorous. Subjective, qualitative, spiritual or creative information that cannot be computerized tends to be ignored, even when it is vital for sustaining manufacturing competitiveness.

The predominance of financial information and accounting conventions have caused many abuses of computerized planning and control and loss of competitiveness by U.S. manufacturers. When computers became available, financial managers had the only mathematical model of the corporation, and accountants had most of the data easily programmed to feed into the computers. Thus financial managers had the greatest corporate bureaucratic power to gain from scientific management methods and facilities.

The equation Assets equal Liabilities plus Net Worth is the oldest, most widely used, mathematical model of business or industrial enterprise.[8] The equation states that the financial worth or scale of the enterprise is defined by summing values of its assets, and that this sum is equated with the sum of creditors' equities plus the sum of shareholders' equities. The equation is also the logical basis for double-entry bookkeeping. Thus accountants have recorded corporate operations as internal and external financial transactions consisting of debits and credits to change the values of corporate accounts, while claiming that their equation is a valid mathematical statement of corporate accountability. Changes in the values of accounts are made in accordance with tax laws and cost-accounting conventions and not in accordance with mathematical logic, for example, as in depreciating financial values of fixed assets or in determining values added to materials purchased and being processed into finished products to be shipped to customers. Significantly, human resources per se are not accounted for as financial assets whose values appreciate or depreciate, only as expenditures, which increase the cost of products and decrease the profits from sales to customers. Thus the mathematical model and accounting conventions for corporate financial management are the determinants of corporate performance or bottom-line measurements taken and recorded *after the fact*.

The assumption that the corporate (financial) whole is defined by the arithmetic sum of its constituent parts is not valid. For parts to be summed and truly equal to the whole, they must be mutually independent. Thus, for example, the sequential order in which they are summed must bear no effect on their total. The assumption of additivity and mutual independence among organized assets and processes for their profitable conversion and sales of products have always been accepted because of necessities for analytical convenience and consensus by markets about measures of financial accountability for the results of corporate operations.

However, the whole equals the sum of its parts is not a valid premise for mathematical models, plans or controls of current and future operations. By their legal charter, their technical design and construction, or by definitions of their socioeconomic goals, their legal roles or missions, constituent parts, products and processes of the firm are *mutually dependent*. Their mathematical relationship to the corporate whole is not simply additive; in fact this relation is so complex as to defy valid, mathematical definition. Modern society has become more organized precisely because the effectiveness of corporate enterprise is greater than the effectiveness of all its parts acting independently. If constituent parts of the firm are not mutually dependent and do not behave *synergistically*, then the enterprise cannot survive long.

Prior to computers, the work of bookkeeping and accounting had much less effect on the work of planning and controlling manufacturing operations. Knowledge of the result of past experiences was summarized and published too slowly, too infrequently and too expensively for much use in managing current and future activities. Management's plans consisted much less of mathematical formulas and much more of personally negotiated, corporate consensus and transactions by those responsible for determining the goals and resources and for designing work processes with those responsible for the work of making products of the right quality available just in time for customers' needs and desires.

However, computerized financial-management information systems have retained the assumptions of mutually independent relations among corporate assets, processes and products as well as accountants' principles and conventions for measuring the parts and the whole corporate status or performance. Memory storage banks have expanded, data retrieval and processing speeds have increased and costs have decreased dramatically. Thus mathematical models and programs, expense budgets, income and cash flow (based on assumptions of additivity and mutual independence) have been computerized to plan, measure and compare the actual performance with the plans and, accordingly, to transmit the information needed for corrective actions. Ironically, such systems are held to be more efficient or effective, because the availability of computer information eliminates or reduces the need for time-consuming managers' meetings for planning operations. Yet, those meetings are needed more than ever, because of the computerized planning systems: first, because they are based on the invalid assumptions of additive and mutually independent relations among corporate assets and processes and second, because they facilitate centralized technocratic methods as substitutes for the democratic methods of management always necessary for combining technical and economic objectives with human and moral objectives sought by the corporation.

Many analysts have noted the apparent contrast between U.S. manufacturers' investments and preoccupations with the short term and foreign manufacturers' commitments to long-term goals and processes. And there is evidence to validate this contrast, as will be discussed. I wish to note here, that U.S. manufacturers' growing preoccupation with computerized financial management information (in other words, with increasing aggregations of different corporate entities) for real-time, on-line planning and control has probably been a major cause of their emphasis on short-term financial investments. In any event, American manufacturers' failure to improve their productivity and to sustain their product quality and process improvement has become clear. And it is also clear that needs and opportunities for such improvements are not revealed, but deceptively denied by advocates of computerized financial and accounting (bottom-line) information systems.

MANAGING HUMAN RESOURCES AS EXPENSES (NOT ASSETS) AND INVENTORIES AS ASSETS (NOT AVOIDABLE COSTS OF LOST COMPETITIVENESS OR PRODUCTIVITY)

Financing, accounting and management require that human resources be planned and controlled as expenses to be minimized so that profits are maximized and that inventories be accounted for as assets, the values of which include labor expenses, i.e., values added according to accountants' conventions.

Operational accounting and management require that inventories in process be minimized so that productivity and product quality are maximized, product innovations are accelerated and competitiveness is sustained; furthermore, human resources need to be accounted for and used as assets, whose values are not diminished by temporary necessary idleness required to serve customers' needs.

Amid their preoccupations with financial-management information systems, U.S. manufacturers have declined, because they have failed to confront and resolve the conflict between the financial management of profitability and the operational management of corporate productivity. Again, top executives have allowed financial managers to prevail: Their data adds up easily and speedily to bottom-line concerns for corporate profitability. But operations managers' concern for productivity and competitiveness could not easily or speedily be processed into a measure of total (overall) corporate goals and performance accountability. Productivity has remained a departmental or functional objective and the measure of performance by managers or superintendents of purchasing, parts-machining, subassemblies and final assembly. And corporate productivity was achieved by maximum utilization (and minimum idleness) of production resources in each department, not by providing products with minimum waiting, just in time for customers' needs.

Thus to achieve corporate financial goals, U.S. manufacturers unnecessarily created huge inventories as an effort to avoid idle labor expenses (to enable workers paid via piece rate, wage incentives to work as productively as possible), to keep production machines operating at maximum capacity and to produce components and products with acceptable quality with minimum work stoppages (which would be required and tolerated if production with zero defects or perfect quality had been departmental or corporate goals). Ironically, costs of lost competitiveness, caused by those inventories, have been ignored including cash unnecessarily tied up in work in process and finished goods inventories; excessive production-processing (lead) time, because those inventories "clog" or delay flows of materials; longer than necessary delays in serving customers' needs for existing products, or for new product innovations; and providing customers with products of acceptable (instead of perfect) quality (i.e., zero defects) and, thereby, incurring the unnecessary cost of customers' complaints, product maintenance and supply services and product returns.

There are other common examples of the abuse of financial management information for planning cash flow and profit and causing decline in competitiveness.

FINANCING QUARTERLY PAYMENTS OF DIVIDENDS OR TAXES

In manufacturing firms a widespread practice has been to liquidate inventories or to reduce quantities or materials received from suppliers to raise the cash needed for quarterly payments of dividends to shareholders or corporate income taxes. From the financial manager's point of view, such actions are preferred, because short-term loans with high interest rates mean adverse effects on cash flow and corporate profit. But from the operations managers' viewpoint, reducing inventories and deliveries from suppliers disturbs the flow of materials and products just in time for customers and jeopardizes quality assurance capabilities of manufacturing processes. The cost of these disturbances may be much higher than the financial cost of the interest on a loan taken to avoid liquidating inventories or disturbing the flow of materials or the use of suppliers and employees.

However, the financial managers' computerized projections of cash flow affecting profit and of the interest cost of the loans to fund dividends are much more easily quantified to convince the chief manufacturing executive. Purchasing, production, distribution and marketing managers have no such integrated information system for managing the flow of materials and products and corporate productivity and the cost of disrupting the flow is not as easily or quickly quantified and, hence, less convincing to top executives. But, the cost of the disruption of the dedication, work and morale of a majority of personnel concerned with the growth of productivity for customers is, nevertheless, sustained; and its effects are lost competitiveness and more significant economic loss than the cost of the loans to pay taxes or dividends.

TOP MANAGERS' ATTITUDES AND CONCERNS FOR PRODUCTIVITY AND PROFITABILITY

The general manager of a military electronic equipment division of a large manufacturing firm noted that from 50 to 70 percent of the monthly shipments (measured in dollars) were made regularly during the last week of each fiscal month. As a former manager of financial accounting, he could not understand why this end-of-the month surge in shipments had occurred every month during the three years since he had assumed the responsibility of general manager. So he requested the advice of a consultant on operations management.[9]

Defense contracts called for shipments as soon as officially authorized by resident inspectors employed by the Department of Defense, who certified that the equipment was of acceptable quality. The consultant's examination of official Pentagon documents confirmed that end-of-the-month surges in shipments did, in fact, occur. His interviews with the managers and supervisors of the purchasing, engineering, traffic, parts-manufacturing and final assembly departments revealed that delays frequently occurred because of engineering changes in product or process specifications. But the time pattern of those changes and delays bore no correlation with the end-of-the-month surges in shipments. The consultant also examined expediting procedures and found no evidence of delays or surges correlated with those of the monthly shipments.

Then the consultant reviewed the general manager's practices. At the end of the first week of each month he held a meeting as soon as his accountants could compile and distribute comparisons of budgeted with actual revenues and expenses for each operating department. Accordingly, at each monthly meeting, the general manager praised or criticized the performance of operations managers. Also at that meeting, a budget of revenues and expenses expected by the end of the next (current) month was discussed and agreed by division operations managers and the general manager, who paid little attention to operations during the fiscal month.

The consultant concluded that the general manager's conduct was the cause of the month-end surges in shipments, and that as the general manager disciplined his subordinate operations managers, they, accordingly, disciplined their subordinates. Their attention to expediting work flow during the first two weeks was relaxed and then intensified during the third week and became most intensive as the month-end deadline approached. Thus, result of their performance for the month was a reflection of the general manager's attitude and behavior during the month.

The computerized financial-management information system was not capable of more rapid collection, processing and distribution of the comparisons of budget with actual expenses and revenues more frequently than at monthly intervals. The system required one week into the next month to tabulate comparisons for each operating department and for these comparisons to be made available for the general manager's use as the agenda for his meeting with operations managers. So the consultant advised the general manager to focus his attention on easily computed variations in daily and weekly shipments and to demonstrate to his subordinates that he was no longer solely concerned with month-end profits.

The general manager acted on this advice. Within three

months, the end-of-the-month surges in shipments ceased. Both profitability and productivity significantly improved, because operations managers were recognized and rewarded for greater consistency in controlling the daily and weekly flow rates (instead of monthly rates) of materials and products through process operations. Expenses caused by idleness or sloppy work during the first weeks, as well as from overtime, materials expediting and job interruptions during the last weeks of the fiscal month, were eliminated—all because the general manager shifted and demonstrated his concern for manufacturing productivity as the prerequisite means for manufacturing profitability.

CORPORATE GROWTH VIA FINANCIAL CONGLOMERATION AND DIVESTITURE

The predominant use of computerized financial-management information systems to plan and control internal operations has led U.S. manufacturers to use investment market information and widespread adoptions of corporate growth strategies for financial conglomeration and divestitures.

About 30 years ago, chief executive officers Royal Little, of Textron, and Harold Geneen, of ITT, used computers to manage their corporate financial conglomerations. It was said that such a strategy not only enabled more rapid growth of corporate financial power, it also minimized the risks of federal government intervention and enforcement of antitrust regulations likely to result from growth in corporate operations or shares of product markets. During recent years, those risks have declined, because of political changes in Washington and lost competitive abilities of U.S. manufacturers. Yet a larger number of U.S. manufacturers has invested more in corporate financial conglomeration and less in operation growth in U.S. product markets.

Scholars have correctly explained this trend, citing the U.S. executives' preference for short-term (financial) instead of long-term (operational) results of corporate growth processes. But, as noted earlier, computerized financial-management information systems have for a long time reinforced that preference, and in recent years the computerized systems have acquired an aura of scientific rigor, because they process much more relevant, empirical data so quickly. And they have been expanded to include mathematically programmed criteria for making decisions to buy or sell financial securities. Consequently, manufacturing executives have focused more on external opportunities for growth in cash flow in and out of financial markets and less on long-term commitments to product quantity flow or product-quality innovations necessary to improve competitive standing.

Professor Robert Reich described such preoccupations with financial growth as "paper entrepreneurship."[10] Surely, these preoccupations accentuate contrasts in manufacturing executives' financial versus operational performance accountability: economic growth, or financial progress, *without* industrial growth of social institutional progress. American managers' neglect of the requirement of the industrial security of their firm has surely been induced by paper entrepreneurship. Productivity growth and competitiveness in product markets are *prerequisites* for the financial growth and economic security of U.S. manufacturers, not vice versa. Moreover, operational growth and competitive capabilities build stronger, more profitable bonds of interdependence with service industries and government in the United States and in international markets.

Thus the capital funds and human talents needed for product and process innovations or for sustaining customers' loyalty have been diverted to acquire financial control of other corporations. Then, corporate conglomerates are "restructured," a euphemism meaning that their employees (workers, managers and technical staff) are dismissed or that product divisions are sold to generate cash in-flow and sustain the process of financial conglomeration and decline in U.S. manufacturing.

The assessment of the criminal corruption, violation of freedom, the need for revising or regulating investment banking, corporate financial management, or securities market transactions is beyond the purpose and scope of this book. But it seems necessary to try to persuade the reader that overindulgence in the financial management of cash flow within and among firms has been a major cause of the decline, not just in U.S. manufacturing security and competitiveness, but in political, economic, industrial and military security of all Americans. The "greenmail" and "golden parachutes" created by such indulgence signify greed or a decline of professional ethics and dedication by American manufacturing managers, perhaps even their betrayal of all Americans. Let us now consider another kind of controllable cause of U.S. manufacturers' decline.

ORGANIZATION AND DEVELOPMENT OF HUMAN RESOURCES

Excess Bureaucracy, Hierarchy and Technocracy

For nearly a century, U.S. manufacturers have served as the wellspring for expanding scientific management. Its essential characteristic has been the proliferation and growth in the power of special interests, because the *knowledge* of science has had to become narrower and deeper, even while the *power* of science has had to become more institutionalized while growing more profound. Scientific management has focused on planning and controlling specialized processes or functions of manufacturing firms (e.g., research and development, product engineering, process engineering, purchasing, production marketing, finance and human resources) or on managing specialized intellectual or professional disciplines applicable to manufacturing (e.g., computer information, human relations and organizational behavior, econometrics, operations research and analysis, quality planning, value engineering, logistics planning and corporate strategy).

Today, with very few exceptions, the admission to the employment and practice of management is via university credentials certifying intellectual competence in the scientific management disciplines. Specialized, scientific management disciplines have proliferated rapidly since World War II. Most management specialists are active members of professional associations dedicated to the advancement of special-interest contributions by their members. Thus those associations publish journals, conduct regular meetings and provide employment information services for their members and for industrial firms. Manufacturers have employed scientific management specialists, largely because the specialists offer their credentials of prestigious universities or journal articles of scientific proof of their abilities and contributions. Once employed, they have tended to exploit every opportunity to apply their specialized talents, regardless of the priority needs for improvements of the firm as a whole. Consequently, the scientific management by U.S. manufacturers has affected the proliferation and growth of special interest bureaucracies. Compared with their foreign counterparts, American manufacturing managers have been focused much more on the specialized concerns of their profession, while Japanese or West German manufacturing managers have been dedicated much more to the common institutional concern of competitiveness. And American managers have traditionally changed their corporate affiliation much more frequently during their careers, concentrating on the functional or professional concerns of manufacturing.

Consequently, the power of special interests in applying scientific management has tended to fragment and, thereby, to dominate those of the common institutional interests and general management. In effect, U.S. manufacturing management has been more a practice by conglomerations of applied technocrats or bureaucrats concerned with objective, quantitative data and less a practice of leadership by groups of artisans or humanitarians concerned with subjective, qualitative values.

Objective, quantitative data are the empirical grist for mathematical, or statistical, information processes, magnified by computerized electronic communications facilities. Subjective, qualitative values are imaginative, creative and inspirational; they cannot be quantified, except by conventions or methods of socioeconomic accountability or statistical inference accepted, a priori, as valid and reliable. Yet manufacturing firms are the pivotal institutions of human industrial enterprise. So it is as vital for subjective values as it is for objective values to be manifested among manufacturers' goals, products and processes. Thus it follows that U.S. manufacturers have declined because their organizations and management have become "scientized." Common interests and subjective values sustained by democratic management have been subsumed, or ignored, by special-interest technocratic bureaucracies. It is ironic that managers of human resources and organizational behavior have practiced more as applied scientific specialists than as humanitarians or artisans.[11]

Significantly, case studies, which are not the result of socio-technological experiments, surveys or mathematical formulations, offer the most valid kind of evidence of the U.S. manufacturing decline caused by scientized organization and management. Paradoxically, academics, or think-tank consultants, have often criticized case summaries as anecdotal information lacking scientific rigor or universal validity. The president of Harvard University criticized the Harvard Business School faculty for sustaining their case methods of research and teaching and for neglecting scientific methods and moral and ethical values and did not acknowledge that cases are probably most effective because they reveal information and require proficiency in combining values and information from all intellectual and professional disciplines.[12]

Management is both an art and a science of institutional self-governance, and laws for governing affairs of manufacturing firms must be based as much on human, moral and ethical values as on scientific, technological and economic values. Making, executing or adjudicating laws of government or industrial institutions are case-decision processes. They require enlightened, creative and pragmatic disciplines as well as the scientific disciplines of intellect and practice. For these reasons, the following case summaries are offered as evidence of the causes of U.S. manufacturers' decline from abuses of scientific organization and management.

Lordstown, Ohio, and Freemont, California, Plants of General Motors

After Ralph Nader's book *Unsafe at Any Speed* prompted U.S. Senate investigations of its auto safety hazards and faulty design, GM was forced to stop production of its Corvair model.[13] The Corvair had been designed with its engine mounted on the rear end of the chassis to compete with foreign auto manufacturers. GM proceeded to develop an entirely new, compact Chevrolet model, called the Vega, and reorganized production of the Vega by consolidating factory operations of its Fisher Body and Chevrolet divisions at Lordstown, Ohio, under a single organization managed by the General Motors Assembly Division (GMAD).[14] Accordingly, the United Auto Workers (UAW) merged its two local chapters at Lordstown into a single organization for bargaining relations with GMAD. There were more than 11,500 employees in the UAW unit.

The Vega was designed with "the people in mind," according to GM executives. The unitized body made assembly work easier. The Vega had 43 percent fewer parts than a full-size car, so there were fewer assembly operations at Lordstown. Manufacturing engineers equipped the assembly lines with automatic devices and power tools of the latest design, to minimize the workers' physical exertion and to facilitate their productivity. At that time (1972), the average cycle time per car assembled in all GM plants was about 55 seconds. The Lordstown assembly line was designed to produce a Vega every 36 seconds, or an average of 100 cars per hour. Engineers used a computer programmed for assembly-line balancing, that is for assigning parts and micromotion task-time elements to workstations, so that work-cycle time was the same for all workstations on the assembly line and employees' idle time was minimized. Standard, micromotion time data used in computer programs to balance the assembly line jobs were the same data that had been accepted by the UAW and used earlier to plan assembly work methods of the Lordstown plants. The Vega assembly lines were planned for the improvement and more rigorous ensurance of product quality standards; quality defects and product repairs were not to exceed 2 percent of total production. Workers were to be strictly accountable.

Several months after GMAD's start-up of Vega production there were 2,000 defective cars, parked in the lots adjacent to the factory, awaiting repairs; the problems included broken windshields, slashed upholstery, broken ignition keys, carburetors clogged with washers, bent signal levers and broken rearview mirrors. The number of workers' union grievances had increased from 100 to 5,000. Most were concerned with the unfair speedup of the standard assembly work pace and with the large number of workers alleged to have been dismissed by GMAD's management because of reorganized consolidation of the two assembly divisions, even though those allegations were unsubstantiated. After about six months, 90 percent of the UAW's Lordstown local voted 97 percent in favor of a strike. This was the heaviest turnout of UAW voters in its history. Lordstown employees went on a six-week strike without sanction by UAW officials in Detroit, an action without precedence and against UAW's rules. The Lordstown strike was very costly and it provoked widespread attention.

The cause of the strike was attributed to the fact that (1) Lordstown, Ohio, was an industrial area employing many strong, militant, unionized factory workers in steel, auto and rubber-tire factories and (2) compared with other area employees, the age and percentage of GM Lordstown workers married, paying for home mortgages and supporting children was lower, while the percentage with some college education was higher. Thus GM Lordstown workers were said to be more prone than other GM employees to resort to strike actions. GM executives also decided that first-line supervisors had failed to communicate with workers effectively.

After six weeks, the union and management agreed to end the strike. They negotiated terms for workers' seniority and transfer rights under the GMAD merger of their bargaining units. The union withdrew many unresolved grievances over the rehiring of laid-off workers. Although the vast majority of grievances leading to the strike had raised issues of workers' alienation, boredom, unfair production standards and disciplinary actions, union and management did not discuss or resolve those issues in their negotiations to resume production.

GM executives decided that poor communication with employees caused the strike. Accordingly, their remedy was to hire "communications specialists" to work with first-line supervisors and UAW shop stewards, in the role of "people problem solvers." They also posted bulletin boards throughout the Vega factory and instituted daily plant audio broadcasts of such things as the status of Vega sales, inventory, production schedules and shift changes to keep the workers informed.

The Lordstown strike cost GM $45 million in lost production and sales, not including the cost of repairing the 2,000 Vegas awaiting shipment to dealers and the 6,000 Vegas with quality defects found by dealers and buyers.

Did GM executives learn how to sustain and improve their firm's competitiveness from their experiences at Lordstown? My assessment is that GM executives ignored the necessity of including rank-and-file Lordstown employees in their efforts to redeem their failure with the Corvair. Such redemption was required to restore competitiveness, and it was as important to the workers' as to the managers' personal and professional efforts and pride.

The decision to merge the Fisher Body and Chevrolet divisions into the single GMAD division was probably sound. But the employees were given no information about the decision, its rationale or its effects. Yet, they observed that the managers of Chevrolet and the Fisher division were exerting efforts and spending time protecting themselves from the undesirable demotions or job transfers necessitated by the merger. Similarly, bureaucrats of the two local UAW organizations were preoccupied with their self-interest in the fewer but more authoritative positions within their UAW unit for bargaining with GMAD managers. Thus the behavior of GM managers and UAW officers at Lordstown prompted the workers to suspect and resist, much more than to trust, accept and participate in the Vega program at Lordstown.

To this day, GM executives, UAW officials and academic researchers hold that the Lordstown-Vega failure was caused mainly by employees whose sociodemographic and economic characteristics and self-interest were inimical to the purpose of the GM Vega program. Even though the employees filed many grievances, produced quality defects and went out on strike (because they witnessed bureaucratic conflicts among those with authority and responsibility for planning Vega improvements and because they could not obtain explanations much less participate in planning for those improvements), both GM managers and the officials of the UAW local asserted that the employees' alienation was not an issue in the discussion for the agreement to terminate the strike and resume work at Lordstown.

However, those assertions were probably attempts by both management and union leaders to divert attention from their failure of the obligation to serve their constituent employees' interests and rights to be informed about, and to participate in, GM's efforts to restore the good name of their company and its competitive position, by providing a safe, economical compact-model automobile for U.S. customers.

After work resumed at Lordstown, GM executives added $400,000 to the annual payroll by hiring communications specialists to work with first-line supervisors and improve communications and morale of the Lordstown workers. Apparently, those communications specialists would serve to prevent the employees' resentment from growing and a strike from occurring again. But, those specialists also added another bureaucratic hierarchical link to the already excessive communications link between GM executives and Lordstown employees. It is difficult to expect better communication, fewer misunderstandings or contradictions and, consequently, improved employee morale, because workers could communicate with first-line supervisors, their UAW shop stewards and with communications specialists about human and technical aspects of Lordstown operations. Communication is improved by reducing, not increasing, the links in the chain connecting managers with workers.

The GM Lordstown strike may have been a warning to GM executives about managing human resources for productivity and market competitiveness. Not long after the Lordstown strike, the Vega had to be withdrawn from the market, because of customer complaints and resistance. It seems that GM ignored the warning that without genuine participation by workers and customers (along with expert management specialists), manufacturers' processes and products can be neither productive nor competitive and, consequently, are not profitable.

The experience at GM's Freemont, California, plant offers, essentially, the same lesson for GM and other U.S. manufacturing executives. Briefly, employees' morale and absences and work quality defects made it necessary for GM executives to close the plant, which had operated for decades.

After nearly a year of negotiations with Toyota executives, the plant reopened under Japanese management to operate under a joint-venture agreement. Chevrolet Nova models were to be assembled for distribution to GM dealers. Former GM workers were rehired and their local UAW chapter agreed to new working conditions negotiated with Japanese managers. The joint venture was named the New United Motors Manufacturing, Inc. (NUMMI).

Japanese managers proposed, and UAW members agreed to, plant organization structure and processes for democratic participatory planning and control of all operations. Compared with the former GM organization, the number of the levels of hierarchy and specialized bureaucracies of management were substantially reduced. The executive dining room was closed, and executives' exclusive parking spaces were eliminated. Work rules were made more flexible, and employees formed quality circles, which met regularly to determine methods for improving process quality capabilities and product quality and for reducing inventory and assembly process lead time and costs. Although changes were made in tools and fixtures, no major changes or investments were made in new, automated production equipment or facilities.

After operating about 18 months under new Japanese management with old UAW employees, productivity and the product quality of GM's new Freemont, California, plant operation rose to the top rank of all GM factories operating in the United States.

Instead of adding communications specialists, NUMMI executives challenged UAW employees to expand their vested interest and ability to *manage* (plan and control) as well as to *execute* their jobs of productivity growth and product-quality improvements and also to work to strengthen and increase their job and income security. For NUMMI employees, the intensity, psychological stress, monotony, boredom and physical work pace were probably comparable with those objectional qualities experienced at Lordstown and Freemont under GM management. But under NUMMI management, UAW Freemont employees determined those job qualities and conditions *for themselves*, as participating members of NUMMI management. And the gratification from experiencing those roles and from the rewards of greater job security and satisfaction from knowing about their contributions to NUMMI's productivity growth have been much more significant. Employee absences were reduced, morale was increased along with productivity, because NUMMI managers treated rank-and-file employees as assets to be sustained and developed instead of expenses to be avoided.

After their painful experience at Lordstown, Ohio, and the lessons learned from Japanese management of NUMMI, GM executives invited UAW workers at its Tarrytown, New York, factory to participate with method and tool engineers in efforts to improve productivity, product quality and employee morale. The result was that the quality of work life, productivity and the quality of automobiles produced by Tarrytown rose significantly.

As of this writing (March, 1989), GM had invested more than $5 billion and several years' efforts in its high-tech Saturn program. Saturn was intended for computers, robots and polymer scientists to revolutionize the design and production of 500,000 automobiles annually and for the cooperation to replace adversarial relations between UAW employees and GM managers. The size of the program had been reduced by 50 percent and its technology reduced to present state of the art. Results have not yet been revealed. Yet it seems appropriate to express the hope that GM executives have learned from their experiences at their Lordstown, Freemont, and Tarrytown factories that productivity and competitiveness require technology of products and processes to be planned and operated to serve employees and customers, not vice versa.

Chicago Auto Parts Supply Co. (CHAPSCO)

Chicago Auto Parts Supply Co. (CHAPSCO)[15] manufactured hundreds and warehoused thousands of different varieties of automotive parts in Chicago and distributed the parts to its 30 supply centers for sale to thousands of auto repair shops throughout the United States.

The Chicago warehouse facilities consisted of old, abandoned, multistoried factory buildings. The president recognized the growing "housekeeping problems," the inadequacies of those facilities and the need for a new, modern, groundfloor warehouse facility. Accordingly, he assigned industrial engineers to prepare plans for a new warehouse; materials-handling, stock-storage facilities; and methods for packaging, storing and retrieving CHAPSCO-branded cartons of auto parts. The industrial engineers completed their plans and estimated project costs and labor savings yielding a financial return of about 10 percent on the net investment required for their proposed new warehouse facilities. The president refused to endorse the proposal for approval by CHAPSCO's board of directors; he knew that they would not consider an investment with prospects for such a low rate of return. Consequently, no action was taken for the new warehouse.

CHAPSCO employed eight commodity stock controllers, who developed and operated CHAPSCO's computerized management information systems for planning and controlling the flow of merchandise and cash. There were data links between the computer at the main offices in Chicago and the 30 regional supply centers. Sales data were fed back to Chicago. Customers' accounts receivable and regional stock-item records were updated in the computer's memory for periodic printouts. Weekly replenishment-shipment quantities were computed via a mathematical program, which calculated the latest demand forecast and the optimal inventory quantity of each of the 35,000 different stock items at the 30 different supply centers. The commodity stock controllers were responsible for planning and budgeting shipments to and inventories of the 30 supply centers as well as quantities of shipments to and from the inventories at the central warehouse in Chicago. They developed and used complex statistical correlations of data on auto design changes, vehicle sales and registration, and parts-manufacturers' price quantity and discount schedules, so that inventories would turn over rapidly, while serving CHAPSCO's retail customers. They also programmed statistical allowances for any difficulties Chicago warehouse crews might have in packaging, storing and preparing shipments from inadequate facilities.

Although the commodity stock controllers' computer system for planning, measuring and controlling shipments and inventories was considered effective, CHAPSCO's productivity and competitiveness declined sharply. There was a 20 percent increase in shortages of actual (compared with planned) shipments from Chicago to the regional centers and a 15 percent increase in stockouts at regional centers. Average annual inventory turnover had declined to 1.5, and ranged from 0.1 to 6.0 for the total number of stock items. Consequently, the morale of the commodity stock controllers declined, because they were responsible for planning and controlling CHAPSCO's inventories and shipments. Several resigned because of the frustrating result of their work, even though company executives tried to persuade them to continue their efforts.

The abandoned, multistory factory buildings were utterly inadequate for the growth of CHAPSCO's flow of merchandise. Incoming parts had to be stored in the bulk shipping containers, because building space was not sufficient for incoming parts inspection and CHAPSCO-branded carton-packing operations before parts were stored, pending shipments. Thus CHAPSCO had to manage two inventories of each of the 35,000 parts—in bulk containers and in branded cartons. The storage space within, and access to, the rooms of the three former multistoried factory buildings were so constricted that often the same part had to be stored in several different storage locations. Those constrictions made it practically impossible to rearrange physically parts-storage locations and simultaneously to accommodate contemporary needs to handle incoming receipts from parts manufacturers and outgoing shipments to the regional centers.

The proposed new warehouse was clearly and urgently required for CHAPSCO to remain competitive and for the flow of material to occur according to the commodity controllers' plan— i.e., just in time for CHAPSCO and its customers to grow more productively. But the new warehouse plan did not meet the president's and board of director's bottom line concerns for profitability and future cash flow. Consequently, construction of the new warehouse facilities was delayed for several years, and CHAPSCO suffered the loss of a significant opportunity for the growth of productivity and profitability.

Thus a major purpose of this case discussion is to illustrate and emphasize that although *specialized* management of the systems for material flow, information flow and cash flow may be necessary, such specialization increases the risks and loss of corporate *integrity*. Corporate competitiveness and productivity require mutual compatibility of design and operations of those three systems. If management systems specialists concentrate on their own concerns for system performance, then coordination and integrity are sacrificed and corporate performance declines because the systems become incompatible.

CHAPSCO's industrial engineers planned a new warehouse to meet the needs for operational improvement, i.e., material flow. But their planned savings in labor expenses did not meet the requirements for financial improvement. CHAPSCO's president (or industrial engineers and commodity stock controllers) failed to coordinate efforts so that the plan would fulfill economic, or financial, as well as operational requirements. Instead, the commodity stock controllers' morale declined, inventory turnover declined and profitability and competitiveness were sacrificed—all because the Chicago warehouse became inadequate for operational growth and the plan for the new warehouse was not a coordinated effort by the commodity stock controllers and the industrial engineers.

The new storage facilities, space and handling methods would ensure prompt and complete shipments, with fewer shortages and stockouts and more reliable (competitive) services for retail customers. The new facilities would also enable frequent and accurate disposal of obsolete merchandise and the rearrangement of stock-item locations. Effects would be the substantial reduction of capital tied up in inventory, which could be used to finance the construction of the new warehouse. In other words, the new warehouse improved CHAPSCO's inventory of building space, which could be financed by reductions in CHAPSCO's merchandise inventory needs. Corporate control systems and corporate profitability, productivity and competitiveness would have been sustained.

DELUSIONS FROM COMPUTERIZED TECHNOLOGY

We have considered U.S. manufacturers' decline caused by computerized financial management of cash flow and programmed transactions in securities markets. U.S. manufacturers have also computerized their *operations* management of materials and product flow and process transactions of purchasing, production and marketing and, ironically, suffered a decline. Instead of cases, this discussion will consist of descriptions of computerized techniques and how their abuse by operations managers has caused U.S. manufacturers' decline.

Repressions of Democratic Relations between Managers and Stakeholders

It should be sufficient to mention only briefly the works of Elton Mayo, Frederick Roethlisberger and Abraham Maslow and their influences on management of human resources and organizational behavior. Their concerns for motivation, satisfaction, self-actualization, attitudes and behavior of individuals and organized groups are well known. More recently, computers have been used extensively in managing human resources.

Leaders of industry and government have engaged specialists to design, test, evaluate and use the results of statistical sample surveys of attitudes or perceptions of employees, shareholders, voters and customers, not just to research, but to manage human resources. Questionnaires and multiple-choice answers are designed and tested for validity and reliability (i.e., clarity of meaning to all prospective respondents). Using computers and electronic networks, representative samples are frequently taken of entire populations and the results are collected and quickly analyzed, to obtain scientific measurements of majority opinions. Then manufacturing executives or government/political leaders see to it that those majority opinions are clearly imputed and accounted for in decisions affecting their organizations.

Of course, people freely choose to respond or not to participate in sociometric surveys. And questions or issues are put to detect inconsistencies or dishonesty in responses. Thus results can be statistically proved to be truly representative and to be valid measures of the will or opinions of the majority of the population, with sampling errors controlled scientifically, by adjusting the number of respondents included in the random sample. Consequently, processes for sociometric surveys have become

confused with processes for democratic self-governance, because of the results of majority opinions freely expressed by
people who are very likely to be affected by those issues and
choices posed in the sociometric surveys.

However, processes for making those surveys and for using
the results to govern institutions are *technocratic*, not democratic.
People who respond to questionnaires do not participate with
the specialists who design, test and evaluate the questions and
alternative choices of answers posed and collected for the computer to process. If they did so participate, then the survey and
its results would very likely be more controversial, ambivalent
and certainly without scientific (statistical) validity. Controversy
and ambivalence convey impressions of inefficiency, imprecision
or lack of clarity, which are undesired characteristics and should
be avoided in the management of human affairs, whether governmental (political) or industrial (manufacturing or marketing).
Respondents who select "none of the above" choices or who
write their own versions of issues and answers are almost certainly never counted with those of the "computerized majority,"
whose choice becomes the "rule." Because of the discipline for
random selection, respondents who participate in the survey are
treated unfairly, as if they are (and want to be) mutually independent. The majority of respondents have no opportunity to
hear why minority respondents prefer their stated choices. Consequently, if the majority is a very large proportion of the total
number of respondents sampled, then the majority rule tends
to be administered by managers and bureaucrats with less grace
and tolerance for those with minority opinions or choices. (The
majority rule seems to be more tyrannical and less humane or
civil.) Morale declines, dissention mounts. Both "whistleblow-
ers" and creative entrepreneurs tend to be repressed or ostra-
cized. The wisdom and strength of democratic self-governance
may not only be confused, but seriously weakened by technocratic abuses of computerized, sociometric surveys.

Even after OPEC quadrupled gasoline prices in 1973, results
of surveys by U.S. automobile manufacturers indicated that a
clear majority of Americans preferred larger, heavier cars than
those imported from Japan and Europe. Accordingly, U.S. man-

ufacturers cite those results to explain why they have suffered huge losses of market shares and very costly delays in converting to smaller, more fuel-efficient models for sale to Americans.

But suppose that after the OPEC crisis and before conducting their surveys, U.S. manufacturers had staged a series of major (i.e., highly publicized) debates on television networks with consumer advocates, engineers, leaders of organized labor, safety experts, representatives of OPEC, auto manufacturers and pollution, or environmental, experts. And suppose further that issues for debate included auto safety, economy, comfort, trends in gasoline prices and the effect of the growth in auto imports—as well as size and weight. Although admittedly conjectural, it is nonetheless doubtful that Detroit's survey experts would have designed their survey to have elicited a majority of respondents who preferred large, gas-guzzler automobiles, which American manufacturers continued to produce for too long, or that a majority of Americans would have expressed a preference for a delay in production of more fuel-efficient American cars and a decline in sales and employment by U.S. auto manufacturers. Representative democracy involves arguments by citizens concerned with defining and deciding issues affecting their lives. It is scientific, but it may be deceptive, to rely on results of random samples of citizens who have no opportunity to participate with those who design, conduct and use sociometric surveys as substitutes for the processes of democratic self-governance.

It may be more than mere coincidence that there is an upward trend in the proportionate number of Americans responding to computerized surveys and a downward trend in proportions who vote in democratic elections. During the 1980 presidential election, based on predictions from its computer surveys of Americans who had just cast their votes, one of the major television networks announced, before polls had closed in West Coast states, that President Reagan would win a very strong majority of the electoral college votes. It is impossible to estimate scientifically the number of voters who heard that broadcast and, consequently, decided that their vote could not make a difference in the outcome of the official election. Yet, it is an ironic fact that only 27 percent of Americans of voting age cast their ballots in the 1980 presidential election.

Relatedly, the efficiency and aura of scientific virtue about computers have had ironic effects on educators as well as managers of manufacturing firms. Students are increasingly subjected to objective tests (i.e., true-false and multiple-choice questions) that are quickly and accurately graded by computers. Fewer examinations require students to compose their own answers and to resolve complex, interdependent issues. At the same time, there is mounting skepticism about the intellectual and professional capabilities of the graduates of U.S. colleges and universities. In fields of industrial and public administration and sociology and economics, sociometric surveys, which generate empirical data for statistical analyses and scientific inferences, are much more acceptable as scholarly research for Ph.D. theses or journal articles than case studies of practical experiences. And U.S. manufacturers have come to accept academic degrees from universities as almost exclusive credentials for employment and admission to professional practice as managers of their firms' future progress. Credentials from work experience of their employees are increasingly ignored, even though those credentials, like research and case studies, might provide more valid and reliable indications of potential and significant contributions to the future management of their firms. Moreover, admission to management based on work experience as a nonmanager is a significant act of participatory management and high morale for all employees. Demonstrations of these subjective, human qualities are requisites for manufacturers' productivity and competitiveness just as vital as objective scientific characteristics of manufacturers' products, processes or human resources.

Yet, as suggested earlier, vital commitments to subjective human qualities or organizations and management continue, ironically, to be ignored, because those qualities cannot be computerized. The results of computerized surveys and of objective-question examinations, however, are scientific, noncontroversial measurements of human choices or of professional capabilities freely expressed and scientifically proved to be statistically valid and reliable by specialized experts in the design and conduct of those surveys and examinations. Thus management scientists seem to have placed management artists (or advocates of vital, subjective or humanistic values) in a catch-22 situation. Arguably, subjective human qualities of organization and management processes can be measured from the results of computerized processes (sociometric surveys, objective examinations, etc.). But those measurements are empirical, and their importance or vitality is lost, precisely because they are empirical and extraneous from the processes of organization and management per se. The empirical results of measurement processes are not, and cannot be, powerful, creative, entrepreneurial or inspirational values intrinsic with, and necessary for, effective management of future results.

Mathematical Programming of U.S. Manufacturing Operations

The increased availability of computers brought forth increased applications of computerized methods for planning and controlling U.S. manufacturing operations and decreased applications of human participatory planning and control by U.S. manufacturers. In effect, computers have been used to centralize and separate the power of information for planning from knowledge and responsibility for executing manufacturing processes. Such separation has caused a decline in manufacturers' competitiveness, because computers were used more to facilitate the bureaucratic growth of management scientists than to enable line-operating managers themselves to coordinate their work processes for corporate competitiveness.

Computerized intelligence also accentuated specialized scientific management and the importance of university credentials for admission to the practice of manufacturing operations management. Since World War II, all university curricula in industrial engineering and management, and many professional management societies, have fostered growth of bureaucracies for management information systems. The American Production and Inventory Control Society (APICS) has effectively advocated applications of a computerized method for manufacturing requirements planning (MRP). And journals of The Institute of Management Science (TIMS) and Operations Research Society of America (ORSA) have published articles on linear programming, integer programming, operations networks and dynamic programming of corporate operations.

All these computer programs involve sets of mathematical equations comprising a model for balancing the use of manufacturing resources and processes with customers' demands. Computer systems specialists, or management scientists, design the model and select equations, parameters and variables to describe corporate operations in mathematical computer language. They select criteria for minimizing costs or maximizing gain (profit or efficiency) and technical/economic measures of resource availability, costs, productivity or capacity of suppliers and workstations involved in procurement, warehousing, manufacturing and distribution processes as well as market demands, units and prices of products. Thus they establish in terms of mathematical computer logic, the accuracy or reliability of the model for predicting the actual behavior and performance of corporate operations, overall. In relations among the parts with the overall result of corporate operations, assumptions of mutual independence additivity or certainty are made, tested and verified usually by the management systems specialists, themselves, not by operations managers, whose plans are affected by the model. Their models for managing the flow of materials and products are designed and used in a manner analogous to the way financial-accounting and management specialists decide on computer models or accounting conventions for planning, measuring and controlling the flow of corporate cash.

Yet, corporate operations managers, on their own terms, are making product and process innovations and routine, material or product flow decisions to improve their competitiveness and expand their interdependence and influence with customers and suppliers. Or if held accountable to plans and controls determined by the specialists in management science and computer information systems, then the morale of the operations managers and the competitiveness of the manufacturing firms are likely to decline.

There is little doubt that computer program models of manufacturing operations are effective tools for planning, coordinating and controlling manufacturing operations and for improving corporate competitiveness. Those models relate mathematically specialized resources and processes to purposes and performance by the corporation as a whole; they provide clear, direct focus on priorities (i.e., needs and opportunities) for specific improvements. Thus those models enable managers of product engineering, process engineering, purchasing, production and marketing to work together more effectively as operations managers. But those same operations managers should understand mathematics and computer language so they are the ones who develop, test and use the models. Those models are almost inevitably based on tenuous assumptions about the true behavior or corporate performance of interdependent relations among resources, processes, products and customers. Subjective, creative judgments of experienced operations managers will always be vital requirements for improved competitiveness.

Thus U.S. manufacturers have ironically suffered from a decline in their competitiveness, even though they increased their applications of computerized management planning and control of operations. Instead of requiring and rewarding operations managers for developing, utilizing and improving their own computer models and systems, bureaucracies of management scientists and computer specialists were superimposed to replace or demoralize operations managers and their traditional, proven methods and meetings to improve corporate competitiveness.

Computer program models offer useful descriptions of technical and economic relations among manufacturers' operating organizations. They provide accurate and reliable insights to specify priority opportunities and the means for improving the flow of materials and products to customers. (More on this point in chapter 4.) But operations managers' meetings, plans and controls are still required. Computer program models do not (and probably never will) describe processes for future, synergistic, interdependent relations among people, materials, machines, energy, information and cash for use as a substitute of the plans and controls of operations managers, so that qualities and deliveries of products are always just in time for customers' needs.

In essence, American manufacturers have suffered a decline in their competitiveness, because of their excessive investments in computerized planning and control systems installed more to expand staff and methods of scientific management than to enhance corporate productivity growth. Since the 1950s, computers have been even more widely proclaimed facilitators of management science and increased corporate effectiveness. Without a computer, an American manufacturer was not "with the trend" for progress. So manufacturers employed increasing numbers of specialists with university credentials for practice in management sciences of operations research, social and organizational behavior and computerized intelligence systems. These specialists applied their talents more often on their own terms, than on the terms specified by the operations managers. The language of statistical models or computer software used by management science specialists to describe manufacturing operations created communication difficulties with operations managers. And management science groups themselves developed and applied their computer models to solve operating problems that they defined. Their models affected the flow of materials and products through all functional organizations, so problems of "language," communication and coordination among operations managers and management science systems specialists were made even more difficult.

Thus management science computer specialists applied their models, concepts and techniques, while operations managers continued to work together pragmatically on problems of quality flow, just in time for customers. And, too often, the revolutionary era of computers has caused U.S. manufacturers' decline: Too much of a good thing can be worse than not enough.

The ironies of the computer age suffered by U.S. manufacturers are, admittedly, articles of faith, perhaps, more than facts. So I would conclude with other authors' observations I believe to be relevant.

Intellect is the capitalized and communal form of live intelligence; it is intelligence stored up and made into habits of discipline, signs and symbols of meaning, chains of reasoning and spurs to emotion—a shorthand and wireless by which the mind can skip connections, recognize ability, and communicate truth.[16]

Trust does not reside in exact recording of every detail. It never has. Instead it resides in myths that direct attention to what is common amid diversity by neglecting trivial differences in detail. Such myths made subsequent experience intelligible and can be acted on. Human society is more complicated than atoms and molecules, and scientific efforts to make human conduct intelligible, predictable and controllable have never met with much success. Yet our social existence depends on shared values, symbols and meanings acted upon by hundreds, thousands and millions of persons.[17]

Manufacturing is a human enterprise to make better products for more people, not a scientific process to make more money for fewer people.

NOTES

1. S. W. Sanderson, "American Industry Can Go Home Again," *Across the Board* (February 1986): 38.

2. D. B. Thompson, "Exodus: Where is U.S. Industry Going?" *Industry Week*, January 6, 1986, p. 28.

3. *The New York Times*, October 19, 1988, p. A1.

4. D. F. Mitchell, "Some Firms Resume Manufacturing in U.S. After Foreign Fiascoes," *The Wall Street Journal*, October 14, 1986, sec. 1, pp. 1, 26.

5. K. Dreyfack, "Even American Motors Knowhow is Headed Abroad," *Business Week* (March 3, 1986): 62.

6. Norman Jonas, "The Hollow Corporation," *Business Week* (March 3, 1986): 58.

7. Marc Uri Porat, *The Information Economy*, 9 vols. (Washington, D.C.: U.S. Department of Commerce, 1977). R. Hamrin, *Managing Growth in the 1980's* (New York: Praeger, 1980) lists 14 components of the U.S. information industry that earned $702.8 billion in revenue during 1975.

8. Lucia Paciolo published *Summa de Arithmetica Geometrica, Proportioni et Proportionalita* in 1484, according to A. C. Littleton, *Accounting Evolution to 1900* (New York: American Institute Publishing Co., 1933).

9. Summaries of the author's professional consulting experiences are described in greater detail in G. K. Chen and R. E. McGarrah, "Aerospace Electronic Systems, Inc.," in *Productivity Management: Text and Cases* (New York: CBS, Dryden Press, 1982), 164–173.

10. Robert B. Reich, *The Next American Frontier* (New York: Penguin Books, 1983), Chapt. 8.

11. Contributions by management specialists in human relations and organizational behavior have grown more controversial. The School of

Organization and Management, Yale University, dismissed six, nontenured faculty specialists in these fields, according to James R. Norman, "Days of Rage at Yale B-School," *Business Week* (December 12, 1988); Alison Leigh Cowan, "New Dean's Proposals Raise Fears in a Yale Department," *The New York Times*, October 30, 1988, sec. C, p. 40.

12. *The New York Times* summarized President Derek Bok's report to Harvard's Board of Overseers in Gene Maeroff, "Harvard: A Case Study," May 6, 1979, p. D3.

13. Ralph Nader, *Unsafe at Any Speed* (New York: Grossman, 1965).

14. General Motors' experience at its Vega plant, Lordstown, Ohio, was described by Professor Hak-Cheng Lee, "Lordstown Plant of General Motors (A) & (B)," in *Productivity Management*, by G. K. Chen and R. E. McGarrah, 320–340. Highlights of the experience at GM's Tarrytown, New York, plant, were published by Robert H. Guest, "Quality of Worklife—Learning from Tarrytown," *Harvard Business Review* (July-August, 1979): 128–136.

15. Chicago Auto Parts Supply Co. is a disguised name of a real company; the case was researched by the author and published in *Productivity Management*, by G. K. Chen and R. E. McGarrah, pp. 233–262.

16. Jacques Barzun, *The House of Intellect* (New York: Harper & Brothers, 1959).

17. William MacNeil, "Make Mine Myth," *The New York Times*, December 28, 1981, sec. A, p. 19.

3

U.S. Manufacturers' Decline: External Causes

The focus of this discussion is on Washington's policies for U.S. security in international affairs. The reader will recall explanations in chapter 1 that national governments must depend substantially on manufacturing firms for their security, power and status in international relations with other governments. And in chapter 2, mention was made of conflicting effects on U.S. manufacturers' competitiveness and national security of Washington's policies for civil/industrial growth and military/industrial growth.

Although this chapter is nominally concerned with external causes of their decline emanating from Washington's policies, in no way is the title of this chapter intended to excuse U.S. manufacturers from their efforts to reform Washington's policies and improve U.S. national security. The U.S. is a democracy governed by, for and of enlightened self-interests of its citizens and institutions. Therefore, the causes of U.S. manufacturers' decline expounded in this chapter are intended as provocations for reform efforts to be exerted as much by the leaders of American business and industry as by statespeople and politicians in Washington.

Leaders of government and industry are debating whether the United States needs a national industrial policy. If so, should it be to accelerate growth of high-tech industries, to revive growth of our smokestack industries, or to rebuild our public facilities for transportation, water resources and waste management and education?

Questions of industrial policy should be addressed as issues of national security, and questions of national security should be considered matters of industrial policy. For ours is an industrial civilization in which industrial and economic growth is the ethic of survival of institutions and nations. For the past 300 years, industry has stimulated and responded to peoples' rising expectations by exploiting science and technology. Whether socialist or capitalist, every nation depends on industrial/economic growth.

Unless there is a change from well-established U.S. policies for military/industrial growth and national security, the outcome of the debate on national industrial policies and the means for restoring manufacturers' competitiveness will be of little significance. More important, the security of Western democracies very likely will be jeopardized. Healthy industrial competition and growth in political and economic interdependence are what the security of Western democracies is essentially about. As one authority has stated, "Maintaining adequate security and conducting successful arms negotiations will be difficult without healthy and substantial harmony among allies."[1] America's conduct of military or industrial affairs has raised trade deficits, public and private financial indebtedness, and decreased U.S. manufacturers' competitiveness. Obsession with military power for destruction has made too many Americans feel and act as if there is no future; so they borrow and spend for today, ignoring deficits. What changes can be made to strengthen U.S. leadership, manufacturers' competitiveness and Western security?

WESTERN INTERDEPENDENCE, U.S. MILITARY/ INDUSTRIAL INDEPENDENCE AND U.S. MANUFACTURERS' DECLINE

Since World War II, U.S. leaders have been committed to a security strategy of multinational interdependence. The Bretton

Woods Agreement, the International Monetary Fund, the World Bank, the Marshall Plan, the General Agreement on Tariffs and Trade (GATT), NATO, the annual economic summit meetings and, not least, the internationalization of private, industrial procurement, production, marketing and financial operations have made interdependence a reality of Western security. To ensure supplies and technology needed in the Middle East, Asia, Africa and Latin America, Western democracies have made such interdependence global and irrevocable. As noted earlier, commitments to the European Common Market and the North American (Canadian/U.S.) Common Market, mounting efforts toward common, equitable terms for market accountability among Asian Rim countries and the United States and, not least, the Soviet reforms of *glasnost, perestroika,* and initiatives for joint ventures with Western industries—all are valid indications that international interdependence is not just an idealistic slogan but a concrete requirement for political, economic and industrial security and progress by society.

Yet, U.S. leaders remain committed to a pre-World War I strategy of national independence in their conduct of U.S. military/industrial affairs. The Pentagon's procurement policy is almost exclusively to "buy American." Its arms-export policy has been to "sell American" aggressively, in competition not only with the Soviet bloc nations, but often with NATO allies and, more recently, with other nations such as China, Taiwan, India and Brazil.

Several reasons are cited to explain why U.S. leaders resist a policy of multinational cooperative interdependence for the defense industries of Western democracies. One reason is that the security of American military forces would be jeopardized if they depended on European or Japanese industries for their equipment. Because of the geographic proximity of Europe and Japan to the USSR, so goes this argument, European and Japanese industries would be "too easily subjected to interdiction by Soviet military forces."[2]

But such threats are anachronistic. Since World War II, the United States has maintained global, strategic and conventional military capabilities. The U.S. military/industrial establishment has grown as dependent on foreign sources for energy, food and industrial materials as is the civil/industrial establishment. If a war with the Soviets were to occur, it very likely would be won or lost with equipment already produced and deployed by the United States and allied forces.

U.S. military officials have argued that American forces need conventional equipment capable of global missions (in tropical and desert areas as well as arctic regions), while allied forces are confined to regional missions in Europe or the northwest Pacific Ocean area. But this viewpoint is questionable. The protection of the flow of oil and other industrial resources from the Persian Gulf, Asia and Africa as well as the protection of the flow of manufactured and farm products across the Atlantic and Pacific oceans are vital security interests of Europe and Japan as well as America. So the mission requirements, hence the design specifications and operational capabilities of conventional weapons, should be the same for the United States and its allied military forces.

Other unspoken reasons for Washington's policy of military/industrial independence are that this policy is to sustain the competition between the U.S. Army, Navy and Air Force to procure different weapons for the same missions, and the autocratic, secretive power and political, economic and industrial pork barrel controlled by our "national security establishment" since World War II. This chapter is a discussion of the damages to the U.S. Constitutional power of freedom and open democratic accountability and the loss of industrial/economic and military security caused by Americans' myopic persistence with military/industrial independence and global hegemony, while industries and economies of U.S. democratic allies have grown from their policies for interdependence.

Western allies had to adopt a security strategy of military deterrence soon after World War II. Instead of demobilizing, Soviet Marxists demonstrated military means to internationalize communism. During the 1950s, U.S. manufacturers produced most of the weapons for NATO forces, while European allies, with assistance from the Marshall Plan, rebuilt their war-damaged industries mainly to provide for their civil/industrial needs. In 1958, the Eisenhower administration launched a policy for U.S.-NATO arms/industrial cooperation. In effect, this policy was the final stage of the Marshall Plan. It was intended to help Europeans rebuild their arms industries by contracting with their manufacturers to produce U.S.-designed, high-tech weapons in Europe. Europeans responded by cooperating with the United States in producing F–104 Starfighter (supersonic) aircraft, NATO Hawk ground-to-air missile defense systems, the NATO Air Defense Ground Environment (NADGE) system and other weapon systems. Those cooperative programs were intended to be precedents for European manufacturers to gain the technical know-how and for the United States and allied governments to cooperate in financing, acquiring and deploying the next generation of conventional weapon systems. Those programs worked. Hawk air defense batteries and Starfighter aircraft produced in Europe performed as effectively as those produced in the United States and at lower costs.

Those cooperative programs demonstrated the strengths of the bonds of international interdependence created by the consortia of manufacturing firms in the program. During that period (1958–65), President Charles de Gaulle withdrew French military forces from under the integrated command of all NATO forces. He also forced NATO headquarters to be moved from Paris. Yet the French government continued effectively to exert its procurement and financial management responsibilities and French manufacturers, their engineering and production responsibilities in the NATO Hawk program.[3] Former U.S. ambassador to NATO Harlan Cleveland repeatedly urged that the United States initiate additional military/industrial cooperative programs to strengthen U.S.-European interdependence.[4]

However, the Kennedy administration nullified the Eisenhower policy of U.S.-allied military/industrial cooperation, before it could be demonstrated to provide NATO governments with military security at minimum costs and maximum effectiveness.

As the effects of the Marshall Plan, internationalized operations of U.S. industry, expanded American tourism and the payments to U.S. military forces in Europe, the flow of U.S. dollars to Europe had grown much faster than European industries could export goods in exchange for those dollars. So, our European allies exchanged their surplus "Eurodollars" for U.S.

gold. Thus the U.S. credits in dollar payments caused the outflow of U.S. gold, which threatened the guaranteed U.S. gold
price of $35 per ounce and, hence, the value of the U.S. dollar
as the primary currency of stability in international monetary
exchanges. As its remedy for the U.S. balance of dollar payments
and gold flow crises, the Kennedy administration launched the
Pentagon's Foreign Military Sales Program and applied pressure
for NATO allies to use their Eurodollars to pay for U.S.-produced
weapons and thus to convert the U.S. outflow of gold and dollars
into U.S. arms exports to Europe. In effect, the U.S. government
reverted to its longstanding policy for military/industrial independence, which conflicted with its policies for civil/industrial
and economic interdependence with Western democratic allied
nations.

By launching the Pentagon's Foreign Military Sales Program,
the Kennedy administration also acted as if the control of the
flow of U.S. dollars and gold were more vital to American and
Western security than the control of the flow of U.S. weapons
and the competitive pressures of the United States and allied
governments to spread the arms race among Third World nations. At that time, Secretary of Defense Robert S. McNamara,
renowned for his financial-management expertise, was, of
course, influential in launching the Pentagon's Foreign Military
Sales Program to protect the security of the U.S. dollar. Earlier,
McNamara was among the executives recruited by Henry Ford
II to safeguard the security and competitiveness of the Ford
Motor Company, and was appointed the president of Ford,
shortly before becoming President John Kennedy's secretary of
defense. While with Ford, McNamara and other Ford executives
made financial planning and the control of cash flow more important than operations planning and the control of the flow of
product quality to Ford's customers. Thus McNamara had a great
influence on the origin and linkages between the U.S. national
industrial security policy conflicts and the causes of U.S. manufacturers' decline in competitiveness since 1965.

EFFECTS OF THE PENTAGON'S ARMS
PROCUREMENT AND EXPORT POLICIES

Perhaps for reasons of their myopic adherence to their own
conventions of accountability, political economists in U.S. think

tanks, universities and the government deny that the federal government continues to execute a national industrial security policy for military/industrial growth and that such policy has not only conflicted with Washington's policies for growth in international industrial and economic interdependence, but also has caused the loss of U.S. manufacturing competitiveness as well as uncontrolled growth in U.S. trade and financial deficits with Western allied nations. They point out that the Pentagon budget has been only about 6.5 percent of the U.S. GNP, far below what it was during World War II and the 1950s. They also may recall that U.S. recovery from the Great Depression of the 1930s occurred only after President Franklin Roosevelt dedicated U.S. industry to serve as the "arsenal of democracy," beginning in 1940 and that since then U.S. defense spending has had positive, Keynesian economic effects on the U.S. manufacturing industry.

However, neither consumer goods nor industrial goods nor productive services results from military weapons spending. To paraphrase professor of industrial engineering Seymour Melman, "You can't live in, wear, or ride an international missile or antipersonnel bomb. Nor can such products be used for further production."[5]

Workers in defense industries still demand consumer products. Prices, therefore, are likely to rise because a relatively stable store of goods must do for all workers or else foreign imports rise to defray their demands. Moreover, defense industries draw heavily on the limited numbers of skilled workers who are trained for the high-tech jobs. Pressures for inflation increase because federally guaranteed "cost-plus-fee" contracts permit defense contractors to raise the prices for scarce manpower and materials.

Oil prices set by OPEC have commonly been blamed for the high inflation in the United States during the 1970s. But in West Germany and Japan, which import *all* of their oil, inflation rates were about 5 percent. While importing only about 40 percent of its oil, the United States suffered from inflation rates as high as 13 percent.

Each $1 billion expended for defense creates about 76,000 jobs; 92,000 jobs for mass transit; 100,000 jobs for construction; and 130,000 jobs for health services.[6] The U.S. defense industry is more capital intensive and less labor intensive than other industries. Interest rates are forced upward because government must borrow to meet its cash needs. Higher interest rates cause recession in housing and automobile markets where customers depend on mortgage and installment loans at moderate interest rates. Thus unemployment rises in those industries. Especially in metropolitan areas, unemployment rates, percentages of homeless families, drug addictions and crime rates are highly correlated. Thus savings in U.S. military/industrial expenditures and increases in civil/industrial expenditures have become more urgent requirements for domestic and social security.

While stressing that U.S. defense spending has amounted to only 6.5 percent of the U.S. GNP, political economists ignore that more than 25 percent of all scientists and engineers in the United States have been engaged in the research, development, production and maintenance of weapon systems.[7] Thus the United States has fallen behind in productivity improvements and product-quality innovations for consumer/industrial markets. The United States and West Germany each spend about 2.3 percent of their respective GNPs on research and development in private and public sectors combined and Japan spends 2 percent of its GNP for the same purpose. The U.S. government, however, spends 50 percent of its research and development budget on weapons programs, more than four times the proportion spent by the Japanese government.[8] Is it so surprising that productivity growth in the United States has been much lower than in West Germany and Japan?

Leaders of the U.S. security establishment continue to assert that U.S. military research and development expenditures create "spin-off" advantages for U.S. manufacturers in competitive markets for consumer/industrial products. But such assertions have been myths, since Western European and Japanese industries recovered from their damage of World War II. German and Japanese firms use the same technology; indeed, much of this technology, which is often under license from U.S. manufacturers, was originally developed from U.S. military research and development. These foreign firms have used this technology to improve their steel, electronic, automotive and machine tool products so that they outsell U.S. products in the civil/industrial markets of the United States and overseas. Today, only one American manufacturer competes in U.S. markets for audiovisual electronic products. Practically all radios, VCRs, television sets and audiotape recorders are designed and produced by foreign manufacturers who use technology that was developed by U.S. defense contractors 25 to 30 years ago and that was financed by U.S. taxpayers' support of the Pentagon's security programs.

From growth in their business with the Pentagon, U.S. manufacturers have become debilitated because of their exemptions from competitive pressures of open-market accountability required in consumer/industrial product-manufacturing operations. U.S. manufacturers' indolence and lost motivation or abilities to compete are negative multiplier effects of the Pentagon's arms procurement and export policies; these effects must be acknowledged, even though their precise, quantitative (economic) accountability remains controversial.

Both military and political security interests of the Pentagon, Congress and the White House protect defense contractors from business failures of almost any cause. Less than 5 percent of military hardware procurement funds are expended for contracts awarded to competitive bidders under terms of firm, fixed price.[9] To placate powerful members of Congress, labor unions and weapons manufacturers' associations or because of its inability to control rivalries among the U.S. Army, Navy, Air Force and Marine Corps, the Pentagon awards contracts for equipment not truly required for the military security of the United States. According to a study by the Office of Management and Budget and the Office of the Secretary of Defense in late 1976, more than $400 million was being spent to keep 20,000 workers in defense firms producing more tactical aircraft than would be needed, even under conditions of total mobilization for wartime.[10] Those aircraft were produced for the income and security needs of constituents of powerful, Texas officials of the U.S. national security establishment.

Defense contractors risk very little private capital invested in their operations. Pentagon procurement offices authorize "progress payments" of up to 90 percent of contractors' cash needs for operations expenses and nearly 100 percent for fixed capital needed for industrial plant and equipment. Meanwhile, cost overruns, schedule slippages, faulty equipment and fraudulent requests for the Pentagon procurement officials to authorize payment of contractors' expenses have grown to be much more usual than exceptional measures of performance in weapons systems acquisition programs. The Pentagon procurement scandals of 1989 were the almost inevitable consequence of the trillions of dollars expended for military equipment during the Reagan administration. Military operating secrecy inflicts serious losses: of open political and economic accountability, of trust in democratic political processes and of competitive capabilities of U.S. manufacturers to serve American customers.

The Pentagon's arms export policies and programs have also had "negative multiplier effects" on foreign operations of U.S. manufacturers and the U.S. government.

The Pentagon has employed more than 5,000 people at a cost of $150 million in order to promote arms exports and to provide procurement, maintenance, supply, training and transport services associated with its arms export sales programs. More than 90 percent of U.S. arms exports require the Pentagon to provide such support services; less than 10 percent of U.S. arms exports are arranged via direct contract agreements between U.S. weapons manufacturers and foreign governments. According to the U.S. General Accounting Office, foreign governments do not reimburse the U.S. government for all support expenses involved in U.S. arms exports.[11]

In addition to the U.S. government's absorption of such expenses, U.S. defense contractors paid bribes and kickbacks of more than $100 million to foreign officials to promote arms exports. Such payments are said to be a normal competitive way of life in foreign countries. But should it be considered normal for bribes to be paid by two American defense firms competing for a single contract agreement between the U.S. government and a foreign government? Such scandals occurred and strained U.S. relations with Holland and Italy. In yet another case, the Japanese government stopped deliveries of (and threatened to cancel) $1.3 billion in unfilled orders for Lockheed patrol aircraft, because bribes of $7 million had been paid to Japanese officials.[12] Revelations of those bribes led to a change of Japanese prime ministers and a strain in U.S.-Japanese relations.

U.S. arms exports are made, ostensibly, to fulfill U.S. national security requirements for containing Soviet Marxist expansionism or to promote stability and prevent violent overthrow of the governments of nonaligned nations. Actually, however, the Pentagon's arms exports occur as often because the United States competes with allied governments for export sales of arms in order to counteract the effects of deficits in international trade and payments arising from their oil imports or to reduce national costs of weapons development. Governments of nonaligned nations are pressured to purchase weapons from the United States or Western European governments, because their purchases help absorb mushrooming costs of development and production of more technically complex, sophisticated weapon systems. For all these reasons, U.S. arms exports to nonaligned nations grew very rapidly after Secretary McNamara launched the Pentagon's Foreign Military Sales Program in 1963.

During the period 1965-80, the United States increased its arms exports to 42 nations by 50 percent over the volume of exports during the preceding 15 years. In that same period, there was also a 50 percent increase in the number of military coups and combat engagements by the recipient governments of those 42 nations. The governments of Chile, Argentina, Guatemala and Zaire were overthrown. The military forces of Greece and Turkey fought each other using American weapons, as did the forces of India and Pakistan. Overall, the number of military regimes increased while the number of democratically elected, civilian governments decreased. The record clearly reflects a strong correlation between increased U.S. arms exports and an increase in violent change or a *decrease* in political and economic stability in the 42 nations importing U.S. weapons. Thus while the Pentagon's policy for arms procurement caused U.S. manufacturers to become indolent and unable to compete in U.S. domestic markets for consumer/industrial products, the Pentagon's Foreign Military Sales Program caused a serious decline in foreign exports by U.S. manufacturers of consumer/industrial products.

Iran spent $1.5 billion for imported weapons in 1969; by 1978, the Shah had increased annual arms imports to $19.2 billion. The U.S. Export-Import Bank extended more than $1 billion in loans to Iran to finance those arms imports, at interest rates lower than the U.S. Treasury paid to finance the U.S. debt, even though Iran had hard currency credit from its oil exports.[13] One export arms agreement with Iran involved the U.S. Navy's F–14 fighter-bomber equipped with Phoenix missiles—one of the most technologically advanced weapon systems not yet fully deployed by the U.S. Navy. This sale was approved, perhaps as much to provide $80 million of cash needed to keep the Grumman Corporation, prime contractor for F–14 aircraft, financially solvent as to keep Iran secure from military threats by Soviet Marxist forces.[14] In 1979, the Shah was ousted by anti-American Islamic fundamentalists, and Iranian export market opportunities for American manufacturers have been limited or covert since. Throughout the 1980s Iran used American-produced weapons to destroy military forces of Iraq, which used French-produced weapons. While U.S. Naval forces were protecting oil shipments to Western democracies from the Persian Gulf states of Kuwait and Bahrain, Iraqi aircraft launched French-produced Exocet missiles and killed 37 American sailors aboard the *U.S.S. Stark*. The secretly arranged U.S. arms exports to Iran for payments to finance illegal exports of U.S. arms to Nicaragua during 1986–87 caused a very serious breach of trust between Congress and the White House and between the American people and their national security establishment.

Developing nations as a whole purchased 81 percent of the value of all arms exports by Western democracies and Warsaw Pact nations, and about two-thirds were exports by NATO nations and one-third by Warsaw Pact nations.[15] During the 1980s, newly industrialized nations such as Taiwan, Brazil, South Korea and China manufactured weapons that have compounded and globalized the East-West superpowers' arms race, and achieved an 11 percent share of the world arms market. At the same time, they have increased the lethal and destructive powers of conventional weapons and risks of proliferation of nuclear weapons.[16]

Political and economic conditions in nonaligned, developing nations have deteriorated as a result of increased competition in global arms markets. Vast amounts of capital and scarce resources have been diverted from economic development and famine relief. Destabilizing military activities have increased and these have made it much more difficult for Western governments or United Nations agencies to provide assistance effectively for improving public infrastructures for health, housing, food, education and energy in developing nations. And Western industrial firms have encountered more serious risks in their investments to develop resources and markets and to provide jobs. Professor Lance Taylor of M.I.T. noted, "Econometric studies suggest that each extra dollar spent on arms reduces domestic investment by 25 cents and agricultural output by 20 cents."[17] Today, developing nations are facing serious difficulties meeting their interest payments on loans that financed their imports of weapons and other products from Western industries. Many Latin American nations have had to threaten default in payments, because of political crises of unemployment, inflation and economic austerity. Such defaults are serious threats to Western banking and currency systems and also to the security of U.S. leadership and Western bonds in interdependence in GATT, IMF, or NATO. Opportunities for U.S. manufacturers to expand their exports and reduce the U.S. trade deficit have been significantly jeopardized by effects of the Pentagon's Foreign Military Export Sales Program.

It is ironic that present and former officials of the U.S. national security establishment (U.S. State Department, White House Security Staff and Department of Defense) have profited from very large consulting fees paid by Western business and industrial firms for their assessments of "political and economic risks" of unstable conditions in nonaligned nations, because those officials were influential in the expansion of U.S. arms exports to those nations.[18]

Just as ironic are the facts that prominent leaders of U.S. manufacturing firms have promoted and supported growth of U.S. arms exports, which have increased financial risks and inflicted far greater losses of civil/industrial market opportunities in nonaligned nations than the gains U.S. manufacturers realized from the Pentagon's arms exports.

Influential U.S. officials have argued that if Western governments had restricted their arms exports, then governments of developing nations would have imported their arms from Soviet bloc nations. But this is doubtful, for several reasons. First, the industries of the Soviet bloc nations cannot match the capacity of Western industries to deliver weapons, much less to provide both financial and operational support services. Second, and more important, Soviet influence in Asia, Africa and Latin America has never been as effective as Western influence. Most nonaligned nations have realized that Western democracies provide more of the capital, technology, managerial skills and export market opportunities they require for their development and security.

Angola, Algeria, Zimbabwe and even Libya maintain strong ties with Western industries, notwithstanding their ideological differences with Western governments. Egypt and Somalia rejected their roles as military surrogates of the Soviets. And some observers have suggested that, if the United States had been receptive, Cuba might not have embraced the Marxist Stalinist doctrines of the Castro regime. During the 1970s and 1980s, the Cancun conference of nonaligned governments advocated a "new international economic order" in their relations with industrialized nations. Western Europe and the United States have been concerned about their financial loans and about the increasing migrations of poor, economically deprived people to their countries. These have been clear indications that societies of nonaligned nations much prefer political and economic industrial interdependence with Western democracies and also that expanding and strengthening civil/industrial (instead of military/industrial) bonds of interdependence would be a more effective strategy for the United States and its Western allies to contain Soviet Marxist influences from nonaligned countries. This strategy will be expounded in chapter 6. Now I wish to complete this discussion of how and why U.S. national industrial and economic policy conflicts have caused the decline of U.S. manufacturers and the loss of U.S. national security.

Quite unintentionally, it seems, the U.S. government, by its management of military spending, federal deficits, and the supply and demand price of the U.S. dollar, has been working against the efforts of U.S. manufacturers to provide more jobs, higher income and better products for American and foreign markets and, ironically, against common military security interests of Western democracies.

NATO military forces operate and maintain 31 different antitank weapons, six different rifles, three different kinds of mortar and machine guns, and dozens of different types of aircraft and ground vehicles and naval equipment. General Johannes Stehlin, former chairman of the NATO Military Committee, called NATO a "military museum." General Andrew Goodpaster, former supreme commander of NATO military forces, estimated that standard equipment would increase the effectiveness of NATO military units by an average of 50 percent. Because at present, they cannot refuel or rearm on other members' airfields, the effectiveness of some NATO tactical air units would be increased by 300 percent.[19]

Standard equipment would mean a substantial increase in the ratio of NATO matériel and manpower deployed for combat to those deployed for support purposes, thus creating further improvements in NATO's conventional military effectiveness and deterrent capabilities. These would make it plausible for the United States and NATO to renounce their longstanding threat of first use of nuclear weapons against invasion by conventional forces of the Warsaw Pact, to abandon plans to replace U.S. Lance, tactical nuclear weapons and to negotiate reductions in strategic nuclear weapons with the Soviets seriously.

Standard conventional weapons and equipment would also reduce costs. In separate studies, the U.S. General Accounting Office and the State Department estimated that between $22 and $24 billion were wasted annually by NATO governments on duplicate programs to develop, produce and maintain different kinds of defense equipment intended for the same military missions.[20] And, as stressed earlier, the unnecessary costs of expanding and intensifying the East-West conventional arms race among nonaligned, developing nations have been far greater than those avoidable costs of duplicated facilities for arms manufacture by the United States and Western allies.

Western European and Japanese governments have repeatedly demonstrated their preference for arms/industrial cooperation, while the Pentagon has concentrated on growth of its Foreign Military Sales Program. According to a 1967 study by the Rand Corporation, because Japanese firms participated with U.S. firms in production, the Japanese government increased its funding and procurement of F–104–J aircraft by 20 percent.[21] Also in 1967, British firms were offered a fair opportunity to compete for contracts to develop and produce equipment for the Mallard field army communications systems that were to be procured for U.S., British, Canadian and Australian forces. The British government agreed to fund 30 percent of the estimated $200 million development cost, far more than its proportionate share of the total number of systems to be procured and deployed by armies of the cooperating governments.[22]

After intensive competition by the U.S., French and Swedish governments to sell their military aircraft, the Norwegian, Danish, Belgian and Dutch governments decided to purchase the U.S.-designed F–16 fighter-bomber, mainly because the Pentagon agreed to manage a cooperative F–16 production program in Europe. This program allowed manufacturers in the latter countries to participate with U.S. manufacturers in the production of the aircraft for their respective governments as well as for additional export sales to other governments. The U.S. government assumed responsibility and expenditure that neither U.S. firms nor French and Swedish contractors or their governments were willing or able to afford in order to win in competing for procurements by the Norwegian, Danish, Belgian and Dutch governments.[23]

Thus for the past 30 years, allied governments of NATO, Japan and Australia have demonstrated their preferences for the U.S. policy of military/industrial cooperation and interdependence. A U.S. policy that relied on defense industries of allied nations would provide allied governments with the financial and political incentives they need to increase their defense expenditures. Their industries would share in the development and export of high-tech defense equipment to the U.S. market, and thus provide more employment and income for their citizens. U.S.-allied military/industrial cooperation and interdependence would have reduced, perhaps eliminated, costly and redundant arms/industrial capabilities and strenuous political and economic pressure on Western allied governments to compete with each other for export arms sales to nonaligned nations of the Middle East, Asia, Africa and Latin America. During 1987, if the United States, NATO, Japan and Australia expended their same, total aggre-

gate funds for defense and the same percentage of their respective GNP for defense, then simple calculations indicate that
the U.S. defense budget could safely have been reduced by about
35 percent. Thus a policy of U.S.-allied military/industrial cooperation would mean that the United States could have saved
$100 billion from the 1987 Pentagon budget and military effec-
tiveness of conventional forces of Western democracies would
have been increased by as much as 50 percent. Perhaps most
important, the Pentagon's arms procurement and export programs would have exerted far less influence in causing the
growth of U.S. manufacturers' indolence and decline in their
competitiveness in the U.S. and foreign markets. Instead of
growing into a global arms/industrial hegemony, U.S. defense
contractors would have been more efficient, competitive and
productive, because they would have been free to compete, to
consort or to merge interests with foreign manufacturers in cooperative arms development and production programs financed
by the United States and its partner governments. Management
staff of the Pentagon would work closely with counterpart staff
of defense ministries of different governmental consortia organized to finance and manage the acquisition of different conventional weapons in partnership with the U.S. government.
Thus different organizations would reduce the risks and costs
of corrupt, conspiratorial influences by consultants, contractors,
regional political leaders or powerful Congressmen, and reduce
costs of redundant weapons procured because of damaging,
competitive rivalries by the U.S. Army, Navy and Air Force. All
these unnecessary costs have been experienced repeatedly by
the Pentagon, because of the U.S. government's security strategy of military/industrial independence from allied, Western democracies and, of course, because every weapons-acquisition
program has to be conducted in secrecy, with exemptions from
measures of open market accountability, which afford trust in
government programs for acquiring civil/industrial equipment.

　　Thus U.S. manufacturers have declined because of the Pentagon's arms procurement and export policies of buy American
exclusively, and sell American aggressively. U.S. trade deficits
and public and private financial deficits have unnecessarily
grown because of Washington's conflicting strategies for na-

tional industrial/economic security and growth to foster international interdependence for civil/industrial growth and to foster national independence for military/industrial growth.

Washington leaders have ignored this conflict. And their efforts to reduce U.S. trade deficits and improve U.S. manufacturers' competitive standing have also had ironic effects on U.S. industrial and economic security.

WASHINGTON'S MONETARY POLICIES: A CAUSE OF U.S. MANUFACTURERS' DECLINE

In the 1960s, to divert European withdrawal of U.S. gold from Fort Knox and to sustain the U.S. dollar as the firm foundation value for international monetary exchange, Washington officials promoted exports and stifled opportunities and challenges for U.S. weapons manufacturers to compete, cooperate or merge interests with their industrial counterparts of allied nations. In effect, the security of the U.S. dollar for measuring international economic interdependence was made more important than the security of U.S. manufacturers' capabilities for developing and competing in international common markets to serve people of Western democracies. As a result, U.S. manufacturers grew more dependent on the Pentagon for funding and managing their research, development, production and marketing functions, both foreign and domestic; this made them less competitive.

In the 1980s, to improve U.S. manufacturers' competitiveness and to promote their exports to reduce U.S. trade deficits, Washington officials arranged for the devaluation of the U.S. dollar in exchange for the Japanese yen and German deutsche mark. The intention was to reduce prices of U.S. products so that U.S. manufacturers could improve their competitive standing in U.S. and foreign markets. As results, the U.S. dollar value became less stable in foreign currency exchanges, and, consequently, U.S. manufacturers invested more to build foreign factories instead of U.S. factories. U.S. trade deficits did not decline. Japanese and West German manufacturers, using their cheaper U.S. dollars to build or acquire U.S. factories, sustained their competitive growth in, and their exports to, the U.S. market.[24] The effects of the U.S. dollar devaluation also included dual, countervailing pressures for inflation and for the Federal Reserve Board to raise U.S. interest rates, both deleterious to growth of U.S. manufacturers' competitiveness.

As mentioned earlier, U.S. manufacturers' opportunities for export growth and global competitiveness were significantly reduced during 1973-87, also because of developing nations' (mainly Latin American) $1.5 trillion of debt to Western banks (mainly the United States, the World Bank, the International Monetary Fund and the U.S. government).

After quadrupling their oil prices in 1973, OPEC governments made large dollar deposits in U.S. banks, which promptly and rapidly boosted their loans to Latin American nations at interest rates keyed to those of the United States. Funds for those loans far exceeded their own investment management capabilities; so Latin Americans sent an estimated $300 billion abroad to Swiss banks. The U.S. government also extended loans for Latin American governments to finance their imports of weapons, which grew at an annual rate of 12 percent during the 1970s,[25] and during the 1980s to finance their acquisitions of production equipment for manufacturing conventional weapons. Of course, these transactions did not enhance their economic capabilities for repayment of their loans from the United States.[26] Prior to 1981, U.S. exports to Latin American countries exceeded U.S. imports from those countries. After 1982, exports from Latin American countries to the United States exceeded U.S. exports to those countries and the gap in the standards of living was growing out of control. By 1985, political and economic stress from triple-digit inflation, double-digit unemployment, malnutrition, crime and drug trafficking in Latin America had raised concerns in Washington about the security of American loans and threats of total breach of financial interdependence, public and private.[27] Threats of Latin Americans' concerted default in repayment of loans to the United States were considered security risks of the collapse of the U.S. banking and currency systems.

Thus Americans have suffered two ironies from Washington's monetary policies to devalue the U.S. dollar in exchange for the Japanese yen and German deutsche mark and its financial policy to sustain the viability of U.S. loans to Latin American countries. The U.S. government's political and economic bonds with those countries have been strained. U.S. manufacturers' export capabilities have been weakened, not strengthened, and U.S. trade deficits have grown instead of declined, as had been expected.

It is apparent that those monetary and financial policies were formulated and executed without consultations with leaders of U.S. manufacturing operations and without consideration of their adverse effects on U.S. manufacturers' efforts and opportunities to reduce their trade deficits and expand their exports. At both corporate and national levels, executives of U.S. industrial and economic affairs have failed to "get their act together." Financial executives of American firms have acted as if cash flow is more important than product flow. Officials of the U.S. Treasury and the Federal Reserve Board have acted as if the U.S. government's financial and monetary power in the international exchange of currency and credit is capable of boosting U.S. manufacturers' competitive standing and exports. Ironically, neither the industrial nor the economic status of American society has improved. Those executives seem to persist in their ignorance of the lessons to be learned from the examples of Japan and West Germany, whose priorities for the manufacturers of highest quality civil products enabled their growth from the ruins of World War II into world-class, political and economic powers of the 1990s.

For too long, Washington leaders have also ignored (1) the warnings by President Dwight Eisenhower about the deleterious effects of the growth of the U.S. military/industrial complex on American political and economic freedom, strength and industrial security and (2) the loss of competitiveness and growth of indolent dependence by U.S. manufacturers on the Pentagon's arms procurement and export policies of buy American exclusively and export American aggressively. At the present, the U.S. government competes with allied governments of NATO, Japan and nonaligned nations (China, South Korea and Brazil) as often, or as intensively, as with the Soviet-led governments of the Warsaw Pact, while U.S. manufacturers' competitiveness declines.

NOTES

1. Robert D. Hormats, "West Economics—And Security," *The New York Times*, January 18, 1985, p. A21.

2. Personal communication with Reginald Jones, chairman and CEO, General Electric Company, February 18, 1981.

3. R. E. McGarrah, *Study of the NATO Hawk Program* (Washington, D.C.: Logistics Management Institute, 1965).

4. Ambassador Cleveland spoke of cooperative weapons development and production programs as the "glue" required to sustain U.S.-NATO solidarity during several interviews with the author in 1966–68 in Washington and Europe. At that time, political and economic relations between the United States and its European allies were strained.

5. Seymour Melman discussed military economics in two thought-provoking works: *Pentagon Capitalism: The Political Economy of War* (New York: McGraw-Hill, 1970); *The Permanent War Economy: American Capitalism in Decline* (New York: Simon and Schuster, 1974).

6. U.S. Bureau of Labor Statistics, *Structure of the U.S. Economy, 1980 and 1985* (Washington, D.C.: U.S. Government Printing Office, 1975).

7. Committee for Economic Development, *Stimulating Technological Progress* (New York: Committee for Economic Development, 1980).

8. Committee for Economic Development, *Stimulating Technological Progress*.

9. Unpublished findings from studies by the Logistics Management Institute (LMI), Washington, D.C., serving the U.S. Department of Defense on matters of procurement contracting policies and procedures, and contractors' performance. The author served as consultant and vice president of LMI.

10. "Aircraft Industry Found to Retain Excess Capacity," *The New York Times*, January 18, 1977, sec. D, pp. 41, 50.

11. U.S. General Accounting Office, *Improvements Still Needed in Recouping Costs of Foreign Military Sales*, Report AFMD–82–10 (Washington, D.C.: U.S. General Accounting Office, February 2, 1982).

12. R. Halloran, "Scandal Costs Lockheed $1.3 billion in Sales to Japan," *The New York Times*, February 11, 1976, sec. D, p. 76.

13. U.S. General Accounting Office, *Military Sales to Iran* (Washington, D.C.: U.S. General Accounting Office, 1974). The fact that interest rates on loans to Iran were lower than those paid to finance the U.S.

federal debt was not published, but was reported to the author, who served as acting assistant director of the U.S. General Accounting Office, 1974–75.

14. The agreement to export F–14 aircraft to Iran included provision for an $80 million advanced payment by the Iranian government to the Grumman Corporation at a time when Grumman (like Lockheed) was known to be in financial difficulty.

15. U.S. Arms Control and Disarmament Agency, *World Military Expenditures and Arms Transfers* (Washington, D.C.: U.S. Government Printing Office, 1986).

16. Michael Klare, "The Arms Trade: Changing Patterns in the 1980's," *Third World Quarterly* (October 1987): 1257–1281.

17. Lance Taylor, "The Costly Arms Trade," *The New York Times*, December 22, 1981, sec. A, p. 19; Wassily Leontieff and Faye Duchin, *Military Spending: Facts and Figures, Worldwide Implications and Future Outlook* (New York: Oxford University Press, 1983).

18. Peter Stone, "Boom Days for Political Risk Consultants," *The New York Times*, August 7, 1983, pp. F1, F23.

19. Paul Lewis, "World War II Is Over, But the Standardization Battle Has Just Begun," *National Journal* (September 4, 1976): 1248–1254.

20. U.S. State Department, *U.S.-European Cooperation in Military Technology* (Arlington, VA: Ex-Im Tech, Inc., 1974).

21. *Aircraft Co-Production and Procurement Strategy*, Report R450 PR (Santa Monica, Calif.: Rand Corporation, May 1967).

22. As assistant director of the International Research and Engineering Programs, Office of the Secretary of Defense from 1966 to 1968, the author served as chief U.S. negotiator for the Mallard Program, from which the British government had withdrawn. But when the author initiated terms that the British government found to be attractive for its industry, it agreed to fund 30 percent of the estimated $200 million in development costs, and the U.S. share of those costs was reduced by 30 percent, or $60 million.

23. U.S. General Accounting Office, *Foreign Military Sales a Potential Drain on the U.S. Defense Posture* (Washington, D.C.: U.S. General Accounting Office, September 2, 1977).

24. Louis Uchitelle, "Trade Barriers and Dollar Swings Raise Appeal of Factories Abroad: American Companies Turn Away from Exports," *The New York Times*, March 26, 1989, sec. F, pp. 1, 23.

25. Derived from U.S. Arms Control and Disarmament Agency, *World Military Expenditures and Arms Transfers, 1987* (Washington, D.C.: U.S. Government Printing Office, 1987), and earlier editions.

26. Michael T. Klare, "Deadly Convergence: The Perils of the Arms Trade," *World Policy Journal* 6 (Winter 1988-89): 142–168.

27. Susan George, director of Transnational Institute of Paris, "The Debt Crisis: Global Economic Disorder in the 1990s," an address given at Smith College, Northampton, Mass., April 10, 1989; also published in her book, *Fate Worse Than Debt* (New York: Grove Press, 1988).

4

U.S. Manufacturers' Revival: Reform from Within

Initially, we considered reasons why all Americans should expand their concerns about the importance of U.S. manufacturing firms beyond those of economic competitiveness in the United States and global markets. Among all institutions, manufacturing firms are pivotal, because the quality of their products and the productivity of their processes are key determinants of social, political, industrial and military as well as economic security for all Americans. We then considered the causes of U.S. manufacturers' decline attributable to their own policies and practices, and causes attributable to policies and programs of the U.S. government in Washington. We noted that these causes are interrelated and suggested that the interdependence of U.S. manufacturers' policies with the U.S. government's policies should be managed more effectively to safeguard U.S. freedom and security in the post–cold war era of international industrial affairs.

In this chapter we shall consider three kinds of initiative for U.S. manufacturers to revive their standing: (1) to reform their corporate goals, roles, missions and relations with their stakeholders and other institutions, (2) to restructure organizations and applications of their technical and operational capabilities and (3) to improve their acquisition and development of human resources.

REFORMING MANUFACTURERS' GOALS, ROLES AND MISSIONS

Manufacturers may need to invoke and apply a contemporary version of the golden rule: To change society's assessments and rewards for their contributions it may be necessary, first, for manufacturers to revise their own goals, roles and missions to serve society's needs. Accordingly, if U.S. manufacturers decide and act convincingly as if they are in business to make better products for more people and not to make more money for fewer people, then they will have taken a most important step toward their revival. Thus productivity for customers, not profitability for manufacturers, should be restored as the bottom-line, or top-priority, concern.

During the first half of the twentieth century, product quality to enhance customers' productivity was the prevalent, or dominant, concern of American manufacturers. Repeatedly, Japanese manufacturers have acknowledged two major reasons for their ascendance to world-class standing: (1) their adoption of American manufacturers' examples of priority concentrations on product-quality improvements for more customers and (2) American manufacturers' shift in concentration to ways of reducing costs and increasing profits.

Nearly a generation ago, the "Big Three" auto manufacturers of Detroit epitomized U.S. manufacturers' shift of bottom-line, corporate concerns from top-quality products for more customers to more corporate profits for shareowners and executives.

After their frustrations and too-often tragic experiences with the auto safety hazards of GM's Corvair and Ford's Pinto, American customers and voters joined in a political majority to mandate auto quality standards for engine fuel economy and exhaust quality. Japanese auto manufacturers redesigned and produced their engines with improved fuel economy and exhaust qualities, which exceeded U.S. government standards. But instead of redesigning their engine fuel combustion systems, U.S. manufacturers lobbied successfully for less stringent fuel economy standards and simply added catalytic converters onto their existing engine exhaust systems. The result was that American customers suffered additional problems of defective quality and maintenance costs and decided to purchase the more fuel-efficient Japanese automobiles.

The significance of this experience is more than merely anecdotal, in light of recent decades of decline in U.S. and rise in Japanese manufacturers' standing. For it indicates an historical change in U.S. manufacturers' attitudes and relations with American customers and/or voters; and its lesson is vital to U.S. manufacturers' revival.

The lesson is that manufacturers must manage *first* to produce quality improvements for social security or progress and *then* to minimize expenses or maximize revenues for themselves. Whether quality improvements are initiated explicitly or tacitly by customers (real or potential), or whether they must be presumed entirely in good faith by manufacturers, quality improvements are bonds or obligations of morality, accountability and mutual trust. They are also the prerequisite bases for transactions affecting individual and institutional freedom and responsibility, power, security and profit.

Because of their shift of corporate emphasis from quality improvement to corporate profit, U.S. manufacturers have put themselves in defensive, sometimes adversarial roles, vis-à-vis roles of advocacy groups, news media or government regulators, or in their relations with a growing proportion of society concerned about human and environmental hazards affected by the quality of their products or processes. Put another way, U.S. manufacturers changed their attitude toward and treatment of society and customers. Instead of kings or queens, whose needs and desires are grounds for manufacturers' existence (i.e., stimulation, response or fulfillment), real or potential customers have become randomly chosen subjects for surveys by market (social) scientists and sources of information enabling manufacturers to plan profits.

The ironies from the U.S. manufacturers' shift of corporate emphasis to profits are further explained by their increasing reliance on computerized knowledge and their conferral to financial managers priority access and uses of computers for corporate planning and controls. Financial managers and accountants do not think of profits as necessarily derived from the quality improvements that more customers need or desire; instead, they consider profits as derived primarily by minimizing cash outflow for expenses and maximizing cash inflow from revenue transactions. Accordingly, manufacturers' profits have been measured more strictly via corporate financial managers' and accountants' rules for defining corporate goals and measuring, rewarding or punishing operations managers, accordingly, for their corporate performance. Those rules are rarely if ever applicable for defining alternative corporate goals pertinent to different kinds or degrees of quality improvements and then ascertaining opportunity costs incurred because of the differences between financial management's and preponderant numbers of customers' choices of quality improvements. Information is a source of power, and computerized information systems enabled financial managers to expand their corporate power by increasing the speed and quantity of their empirical information, always in consistent dimensions of money and time (or profits). The power of information about quality improvements and sociotechnical needs and desires of more customers was subsumed and increasingly ignored by U.S. manufacturers.

Thus, U.S. manufacturers have lost their competitive standing, because their computerized quantitative planning and controls have been based more on profit objectives and less on quality improvements for people. And they have treated the American public (real or potential customers, consumer environmental activists, investigative journalists and government regulators) more as subjects for sociometric survey measurements, as adversarial litigants or bureaucrats to be influenced by their economic logic or power, than as cosponsors or participatory stakeholders of institutions dedicated to product-quality improvements. Manufacturers assumed a secure role as primary guarantors of social security or progress measured in any and all dimensions.

Understandably, CEOs of U.S. manufacturing firms might assert that they must be dedicated to industrial/economic objectives. They might further argue that to dedicate their firm to the quality improvements desired and needed by society as a whole would be tantamount to transforming manufacturing firms into political institutions, whose purposes must be governmental, not industrial and economic.

However, while acknowledging a consensus about this argument, I must suggest that it is an anachronism. Centuries of industrial revolutionary progress have expanded and interlocked the purpose and process of manufacturers with those of governments, so that both must be accountable to all of society, not just to its special-interest groups. Manufacturers and governments manage their freedom and responsibility democratically, to serve their common constituents, because both institutions are by, for and of all the people.

If U.S. manufacturers consult genuinely and openly about quality improvements, costs and effectiveness with advocates of human and environmental health and safety or with consumer-interest groups, then those advocates will more clearly understand the dilemmas and complexities, and they will have participated in deciding among the values of the quality, the availability and the cost, or price, of those improvements. And manufacturers will have gained understanding about the concerns of those interest groups. Such participatory management increases cooperation and vested interests in accepting the quality improvements that U.S. manufacturers would then produce for their needs and desires. Consultations would engage, not avoid, controversies about individual freedom to differ with mutual respect and common responsibility for consensus, mutual commitment or changes. To be genuine, processes for consultation require patience and urgency about cooperation or competition. Participation would be democratic, i.e., by representatives of manufacturers' associations; special-interest groups; educational, health or environmental institutions; welfare organizations or governments; or by grass-roots, spontaneous efforts by experts of manufacturing firms with counterpart experts of advocacy groups. Thus although processes for *genuine* consultations might not be specific, consistent or efficient, because they should be democratic (not bureaucratic or technocratic), the results of those processes would almost certainly be the improvement of U.S. manufacturers' competitiveness. Directly or indirectly, people and society would be more willing to respond positively to U.S. manufacturers' efforts to understand and fulfill their needs and desires for quality improvements.

Thus manufacturers as well as governments are accountable for their purpose and processes for stimulating and responding to the needs and desires of all of society. Both industry and government must manage their freedom and responsibility democratically, to serve their common constituents, i.e., all the people. Governments are institutions for political, economic, military and legal power that are dependent on, and inseparable from, the manufacturers' power of organized development and the application of science and technology to provide better products for more people.

The attitude and behavior of the CEO of each business or industrial firm should be the exemplary precedents for the purpose and processes of the firm as a whole. It follows that, unless the CEOs of U.S. manufacturers' firms understand and respond to the need for their firm to make better products for more people (not to make more profits for fewer people), the revival of U.S. manufacturing competitiveness and the security standing of American society in world affairs are less likely to be ensured, even though their subordinate, corporate operations managers may adopt other important recommendations (to be discussed later). Moreover, I suggest that it is for the CEOs of U.S. manufacturing firms to join with CEOs of foreign, counterpart manufacturing firms, because quality improvements by manufacturers have raised security issues that are compelling people worldwide to think and act globally and locally about the requirements:

- To protect the security of global humanity and ecology from the threats of destruction of the earth's life-support systems, caused by the greenhouse effect of energy wastage and exhaust pollution emanating largely from products and processes of manufacturers' firms.

- To protect the security of global societies from the threats of nuclear holocaust, armed terrorism, military repression and insurrections caused by secret, unaccountable production, and distribution and noneffective control of use of all the classes of weapons produced by manufacturers.

• To preserve the security of global posterity from the threats of despoliation or exhaustion of the earth's nonrenewable resources necessary for sustaining human life and manufacturers' quality improvements.

For U.S. manufacturers to revive their competitiveness by reforming their corporate goals, roles and missions in society, it is in their enlightened self-interest not just to consult and respond more genuinely (i.e., democratically) about more peoples' needs and desires for their firms' quality improvements. Manufacturers should also advise and convince national governments of their mutual security benefits and requirements to abandon their geopolitical and military destructive means of contention in international affairs. Instead, they should cooperate in fostering common, equitable terms for manufacturers to compete more freely in providing quality improvements for people of developing and industrialized nations. (We shall expound this point further in chapter 6.)

RESTRUCTURING MANUFACTURERS'
OPERATIONAL AND FINANCIAL-MANAGEMENT
CAPABILITIES

American manufacturing firms have lost their competitive power because their goals of productivity and profitability growth have incited conflict more than cooperation by their operations and financial managers. Profitability has been managed by maximizing the flow and minimizing the inventory of cash. Productivity growth, however, has been managed by maximizing the use of machines and labor. Productivity management has focused mainly on increasing the productive capacity or utilization of human and machine processes. Profitability management has focused on increasing corporate returns on capital investments. Manufacturing profitability continues to be a corporate goal. Actual profits are planned and measured, and rewards—dividends, bonuses and raises in salaries—are made after computing and paying expenses and collecting revenues. Manufacturers' productivity is used much more as departmental or functional goals, with rewards for actual performance made according to incentive wage schemes based on productive utilization of departmental processes. In essence, profitability management remains *holistic*, focused on planning and controlling the corporate flow and inventory of cash. Productivity management has fragmented into *specialized functions* of designing, planning and controlling systems to increase the speed or volume of the flow of material through particular processes. It is not concerned with decreasing inventory or reducing the time required for materials and products to flow through corporate operations as a whole (i.e., through procurement, parts manufacturing, assembly and market channels to customers).

It is the conflict between U.S. executives' holistic concerns for profitability growth and their specialized concerns for productivity growth that has caused the decline in competitiveness of U.S. manufacturers. This conflict continued to grow, but it was ignored until Japanese manufacturers gained increasing shares of the U.S. markets for steel, machine tools, automobiles and electronic equipment long dominated by American manufacturers.

Many observers have attributed Japanese gains to cultural differences. Accordingly, Japanese corporations are more productive and competitive because the Japanese society is more monolithic in terms of race or ethnicity and more ideologically dedicated in favor of common (against special or individual) goals and processes.[1] Americans are more diverse racially and ethnically and, therefore, are inherently dedicated to individual freedom and more specialized, professional goals and processes.

Although such observations of cultural differences are acceptable, they do not logically explain why Japanese manufacturers, using the same, basic product and process technologies and rules of economic accountability that American manufacturers use, have competed among themselves and managed to grow more competitive by taking U.S. market shares away from American firms. If such cultural differences are indeed the cause, then remedies for restoring American competitiveness are bound to be too speculative or unrealistic for American executives and workers to adopt.

A more practical reason for Japanese competitiveness has been suggested by the Japanese themselves. They have insisted that they learned to manage quality and productivity of manufacturing operations 35 years ago from Americans.[2] This was prior to the post-Sputnik proliferations and fragmentation of applied sciences in American management of manufacturing operations, a surge that brought forth specialists in information systems, automation, operations research, systems analysis, value analysis, materials management, manufacturing engineering and human and organizational behavior. Japanese manufacturers applied scientific techniques but did not organize, staff and reward as many specialized bureaucracies and experts. Unlike U.S. manufacturers, Japanese management of corporate quality improvements and productivity growth is coordinated, not in conflict, with their management of corporate profitability growth. Efforts to maximize corporate flow and minimize inventory of materials and products are synchronized with efforts to maximize corporate flow and minimize inventory of cash. Such efforts are exerted by mutual dedication of all managers, not by the specialized, uncoordinated bureaucracies and hierarchies prevalent in U.S. manufacturing firms.

Instead of concentrating on maximizing the utilization of departmental processes and minimizing the time and expense of idle machines and labor, Japanese managers concentrate on maximizing the flow of materials and products just in time to meet customers' needs or desires. Instead of treating human resources as expenses to be avoided and inventories as assets always positively evaluated, Japanese managers treat human resources as assets to be nurtured and inventories of materials and products as expenses and costly obstructions of the flow of products or delays of product innovations to be avoided as much as possible.

American managers have tended to increase inventories to implement labor productivity and wage-incentive plans, to ensure acceptable quality and necessary quantities of component parts and products or to avoid costly, yet not irreducible interruptions, of manufacturing processes (e.g., caused by needs for maintenance, setup changes, materials or supplies, or for detecting and fixing quality problems). Japanese managers are much more willing to interrupt manufacturing processes so they can minimize quality defects, inventories, customers' waiting time for products or delays in delivering new and better products. These differences in managing corporate productivity also explain why Japanese manufacturers have been more effective than their American counterparts in exploiting new technology for products and processes, technology that had been researched and developed by American manufacturers engaged in high-tech equipment contracts with the U.S. Department of Defense!

Thus Japanese managers focus their efforts on eliminating the causes of quality defects and minimizing customers' waiting time—in other words, on critical bottlenecks and priority opportunities to serve customers. Such efforts also focus the investment of corporate financial capital more precisely and prudently on product or process innovations that customers are willing to pay for. Once developed, those improvements are installed and utilized more quickly for the customers' benefit. There is less inventory to be used up (and thus to cause delays) before new products are delivered to markets and customers.

By concentrating their efforts on departmental processes and minimizing idle time, American productivity managers focus on technological opportunities to increase process capacity, rather than on needs for productivity growth and quality improvements. Their larger inventories, created because of the efforts to keep labor and equipment fully utilized, must be consumed before new, innovative products are produced and delivered to customers. Consequently, U.S. manufacturers' corporate productivity, market shares and profits have declined because they invested more capital in new technology where it could be applied or in full utilization of existing processes than in efforts toward zero quality defects or eliminating the relatively few, critical bottleneck delays in the flow of material.

Thus a major remedy for U.S. manufacturers to restore their competitive standing is based on two principles. One is that corporate productivity and quality improvements must be planned, measured, controlled and rewarded for corporate performance related only to customers' needs and desires. Productivity counts only after customers have been served by everyone in the firm. The other is that any material or product not being physically or chemically transformed or moved through distribution channels or through production departments is idle, nonproductive inventory. As well-run cash accounts contain only the minimum necessary idle capital, the only necessary material inventories are those at the few critical stages of the process required for the company to serve its customers' needs for the earliest delivery and highest product quality.

To determine those few, critical stages requires the examination of procurement and production-operating data for all processes (suppliers' and distributors' as well as manufacturers' own processes), including production capacity, maintenance time, quality assurance, changes in setups, personal or training needs of employees, etc. and, of course, data measuring customers' demands. Specialized computer techniques such as MRP, optimal production technology (OPT), or linear programming are useful for such examinations. Statistical sampling techniques might be used to obtain data not available from empirical operating records. However, understanding and agreement by all operations personnel on the priority choices of key bottlenecks are necessary, including workers, managers and staff specialists. Authority or schedules for issuing materials and for starting, interrupting or stopping all other process operations are determined only *after* schedules have been planned for the few critical workstations, and the performance quality and productivity of all operating personnel will be recorded and rewarded accordingly.

The amount produced by the noncritical processes during any operating period would not be determined by their respective capacities but by the capacity of the critical processes to which they are linked. Idle machine time or labor time would affect corporate productivity only if such idleness caused a loss of production by key workstations. Thus the flow of products through required workstations, not production capacities, would be balanced. And performance by employees, foremen, departmental superintendents, and specialists in materials and quality planning would be measured and rewarded according to the count of materials or parts found outside workstations awaiting movement from their department. Such a count could be taken at random intervals during planned operation periods. The smaller the count, the greater the employees' contribution to corporate productivity and profitability. Of course, quality defects would also be counted and rewards made for achieving the goal of zero defects.

For this remedy to be effective, work rules would have to be relaxed. There would be less of a distinction between classifications and responsibilities of direct and indirect labor and between lines of authority of staff and operations personnel. Levels of hierarchy would be reduced, because identity with the corporations' common purposes of quality improvements, delivery service and low costs *for customers* would be most important. Provisions in union contracts pertaining to work rules, labor classifications, wage payments, employment and income security would be changed to encourage all operating personnel to work more freely toward the common goals. Employee layoffs would not be correlated with employee idleness but with measures of decline in corporate progress toward zero defects and zero inventories. Human resources would be managed more as corporate assets than as expenses of departmental fiefdoms.

Lower inventories would reduce the complexity and the arbitrary, illogical authority of product cost accounting conventions used to evaluate inventories. Formulas for posting indirect overhead expenses as portions of production costs and accounting rules for direct labor expense strictly as value-added to inventories before shipments are made to customers would lose their significance, because inventories would be substantially decreased to much smaller proportions of the total value of corporate assets. More cost accountants' efforts could then be devoted to economic evaluations of corporate savings opportunities, costs of customers' waiting time and alternative opportunities for quality improvements. These efforts would replace those expended for cost-performance reports, which incite interdepartmental rivalries and encourage departmental investments in equipment, methods and techniques where applicable, but *not where most critically needed* to boost corporate competitiveness or accounting efforts, which focus executives' attention on possibilities for changing methods of inventory evaluations and their effects on corporate tax obligations and profits.

As noted earlier, work-in-process inventories would be planned and controlled as safety stocks only at "key," or critical, workstations affecting corporate productivity and customers' waiting (lead) time for delivery. Such inventories would be analogous to petty cash accounts at different factories. They would be no larger than amounts necessary to sustain the flow of materials for corporate profitability and productivity growth. Safety stocks would be planned according to analyses of past experiences with disruptions of critical processes and of the time necessary to reduce or eliminate the causes of those disruptions. Safety stock quantities would be planned in quantities sufficient to sustain the flow of material during the disruption or delays. Then technical specialists and production or maintenance staff would work to eliminate them. Ongoing observations would be made of the effects of these efforts. If the safety stock remained full throughout a scheduled operating period, then disruptions would have been reduced, and the safety stock quantity could be reduced so it would remain full during the first one-third of the next operating period. This rule, and efforts for improvements at key workstations, would ensure progress toward goals of growth in productivity, quality improvements and profitability. As disruption time is reduced further, key bottlenecks would shift to other workstations. Thus the goal of zero inventory would never be achieved. But product quality and delivery services to customers would continue to improve, because all corporate operations personnel would continue to focus their attention on key opportunities for improvements in product quality and service for customers.

PRODUCTION AND PROCUREMENT SCHEDULING AND INVENTORY CONTROL

The goals of minimizing inventories of purchased materials and work in process would mean that traditional formulas for economical purchase and production order quantities would no longer be used. Those formulas are based on a faulty economic rationale of minimizing the sum of expected *annual* costs of purchase ordering or production process setup changes and costs of carrying inventory. Resulting order quantities far exceed those required by customers during the next time period for production and marketing operations, of say, 6 to 12 weeks. And such large quantities of inventories clog pipelines for the flow of material and prolong customers' waiting time for product deliveries and quality improvements. Thus formulas for economical purchase order or production order quantities ignore management and economics for competitiveness, i.e., purchasing and producing qualities and quantities of products just in time for customers' needs or desires.

Production lot quantities should be as small as possible and based strictly on customers' demand rates. Customers' aggregate demand for products during the corporate lead time horizon should be established as the master production plan. (Corporate lead time horizon is the total number of days required by the manufacturer and his suppliers to process and deliver products to customers.) Then the master production schedule is determined by exploding the production plan into detailed component parts to be produced in the same daily mix for the first month of the master plan. This schedule is derived to produce the same variety and quantities daily, in the smallest possible lot size for each part. Each lot quantity, typically, should be one-tenth of a day's production, so that variations in actual demands are easily accommodated via production changes in small increments. Moreover, effects of queuing delays in processing and transfers among upstream workstations are minimized, because the master schedule has been based, not on production capabilities, but on demand flows in small lots through the critical workstations of corporate processes. The master schedule should then be released to feeder work centers and vendors whose shipping lot quantities and frequencies should be matched as closely as practical with those of manufacturing lots (i.e., one-tenth of daily production). Thus the master production schedule serves as the basis for supplier centers to organize their human resources and to make provisions for necessary vendor materials, all based on daily rates of demands by customers. As emphasized earlier, the only work-in-process inventories are those safety stocks planned for the critical workstations.

Figure 1
Flow of Production and Withdrawal Kanbans

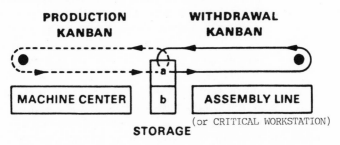

Reprinted with permission from *P&IM Review* with APICS News, September 1981.

Kanban Control Systems

The Japanese shop-floor vendor release and control system, called *Kanban* (meaning "card") system, is highly recommended. It is "paperless" and utilizes dedicated parts containers and traveling requisition cards, which are reusable by workstation operators or material handlers. Thus the Kanban system eliminates the need for additional production or purchase-expediting personnel commonly required by U.S. manufacturers' material-control systems.

Kanban cards are of two types. The production Kanban authorizes the manufacture of a container of material. The withdrawal Kanban authorizes the withdrawal and movement of the material. The number of pieces in a container never varies for a given part number. When production rates change, because demand rates have changed, containers are added or deleted.

The flow of production and withdrawal Kanbans are illustrated in figure 1. The machine center is making two parts, A and B, which are stored in standard containers next to the work center. When the assembly line (or critical workstation) starts to use part A from a full container, the operator takes the withdrawal Kanban from the container and goes to the machine center storage area. He finds a container of part A, removes the production Kanban and replaces it with the withdrawal Kanban, which authorizes him to move the container. The liberated production Kanban is then placed in a rack by the machine center, as a work authorization for producing another lot of part A. Parts are manufactured in the order in which cards are placed in the rack.

The same controls are used to authorize vendor shipments, when both customer and vendor use the Kanban system. The withdrawal Kanban serves as the vendor release/shipping authorization and the production Kanban at the vendor's plan regulates his production.

The effectiveness of the Kanban system hinges on everyone doing exactly what is authorized and following procedures explicitly. As noted, the Japanese use no production coordinators or expeditors on the shop floor, relying entirely on the shop foreman to ensure compliance. Of course, cooperative attitudes and participation by workers are essential.

Results of this system have been impressive. Jidosha Kiki, a Bendix affiliate making automotive braking components in Japan, installed the Kanban/just-in-time system, at the urging of one of their customers, Toyota. Within two years they had doubled productivity, tripled inventory turnover to 30 times per year, and substantially reduced overtime and space requirements.[3]

The Japanese Kanban/just-in-time system makes inventory control relatively simple. With minor exceptions, there are no storerooms. Incoming materials go directly to their appropriate workstations. What little work-in-process inventory exists is stored next to the production centers for critical workstations or initial workstations for incoming vendor materials with higher quantities and lower frequencies than those of manufacturing materials.

The system also requires more intensive focus on so-called indirect works of quality assurance, preventive and remedial maintenance and process setup changes. Kanban quantities of materials are 100 percent perfect and the product quality standards and process quality capabilities, together with methods of quality assurance (inspection), are carefully planned so that production processes are stopped after a single defect is discovered. Methods of setup changes and maintenance are planned as carefully as methods of direct, repetitive production operations, because setup and maintenance work affect product quality and delivery services for customers. Toyota engineers reduced the time for changing setups of an 800 ton multistation press from more than 8 hours to 10 minutes, in order to improve delivery services to customers. Thus if U.S. manufacturers are to revive their corporate competitiveness, then they should adopt procurement, production and inventory control systems that are focused on the flow of materials and products just in time for the customers.

Because of their greater distance from the U.S. market, foreign-based manufacturers would require more lead time for serving the needs of American customers and, therefore, would lose competitive positions and market shares. U.S. manufacturers known to have applied these principles and procedures have accelerated growth in their inventory turnover rate and productivity to levels 4 to 10 times those they experienced during the 1970s.[4] Because Japanese productivity growth rates have been about 4 or 5 times those of American manufacturers and because American productivity levels, in total, are still about equal to those of the Japanese, it follows that application of these principles would enable American manufacturers to match or exceed Japanese capabilities.

MANAGING QUALITY INNOVATIONS

Initial recommendations in this chapter were for CEOs and U.S. manufacturers to reaffirm the principal corporate objectives of quality improvements for more customers and then to demonstrate this reaffirmation via corporate policies for treating satisfied or irate customers, expert advocates of human and environmental health and safety, government regulators, investigative journalists and public interest groups more as participatory managers of quality improvements and less as adversarial litigants or as subjects for deterrence or manipulation via sociometric surveys, public relations and lobbying campaigns. Our second proposal was that U.S. manufacturers focus efforts of their operations managers (including their suppliers) and financial managers consistently, holistically and democratically (instead of bureaucratically or technocratically) on corporate productivity growth synchronized with profitability growth.

Consistent with emphasizing quality improvements for customers and corporate integrity in managing the inventory and flow of cash and materials, our next recommendation is for staff experts in customer relations and product maintenance; in manufacturers' process engineering design and product research design; and in development and testing to work *simultaneously* (instead of *sequentially*) *together* on plans and controls for more rapid and effective quality improvements.

Historically, manufacturers' quality innovations have evolved from a five-stage process of sequential efforts by functional/technical specialists: (1) examining and evaluating the research and technology of others (universities, government, industrial competitors and noncompetitors); (2) developing and testing the validity, reliability and safety of the proposed innovations for the firm; (3) product-design specifications; (4) process-design and quality-assurance specifications and (5) market research and evaluations of users' operational and maintenance experiences. Often stage 5 established precedents for repeating the process cycle for further quality improvements. The cycle time for this five-stage process determined the manufacturer's lead time, speed or rate of quality improvements for customers. Thus managing to reduce the lead time of the process for quality improvements is consistent with management corporate productivity to minimize inventories and lead time for the production process. And improving quality and providing more rapid delivery for customers are almost certain to boost manufacturer's competitiveness.

Accordingly, by requesting and arranging for those technical specialists to work together simultaneously and democratically (instead of sequentially and bureaucratically), U.S. manufacturers can revive their competitive standing. This recommendation is not without precedence. CAD-CAM programs effectively and simultaneously perform stages 3 and 4 of the quality innovation process. These computer programs enable the manufacturers to design products and processes quickly in accordance with customers' specific desires for product-quality characteristics, provided the specific characteristics are varieties within limits of the standard parameters of product and process technologies used by the manufacturer. Thus this recommendation would involve a "humanized expansion" of CAD-CAM system programs for quality innovations.

The technical specialists would engage in dialogue, raising and deciding issues of technical, economic, human and social concerns to each stage of the quality-planning process. The results would be the same, detailed specifications for product, process, quality assurance, product operation and maintenance. However, those specifications would have been accepted and enacted more productively (i.e., holistically), because instead of planning a sequential part or stage of the process for managing quality innovations each and every specialist would have planned each and every stage of the process. Each would have gained and shared both common and special vested interests in the manufacturer's quality-improvement process and its total effectiveness. Consequently, the time for planning and executing quality improvements would be reduced and their effectiveness would be increased.

In essence, this proposal is for U.S. manufacturers to organize and manage quality improvements by requiring technical or functional specialists to act with explicit, interdependent responsibility for achieving the holistic, corporate objectives of better products for more customers. If vital, specialized contributors are made responsible for the corporate whole, then the value of the corporate whole is much more likely to be greater than the sum of the specialized contributors' efforts applied sequentially or independently.

Some readers may infer that this proposal is tantamount to organizations for project or program management. But this is not so intended. Whether for military or civil product improvements, programs or projects have usually been organized so that the work relationships between researchers, designers, planners and evaluators have remained specialized and sequential for the duration of the program or project. The lead time for product innovations by U.S. manufacturers of defense products and consumer/industrial products has grown longer than that of their foreign counterparts; consequently, the effectiveness of U.S. product innovations has declined.

Manufacturers' product innovations must reflect creativity and imagination as well as technological validity and reliability. If technical specialists work together democratically on all challenges and opportunities, then their innovation processes are more likely to be entrepreneurial and their product innovations, more creative or competitive.

Quality capabilities of producers and customers must be 100 percent in accord with quality specifications of designers. And zero defects must be an absolute standard for manufacturers' procurement, production and distribution processes.

During recent decades, U.S. manufacturers have deliberately produced units for scrap or rework. Pressures to avoid idle labor costs, to operate piece-rate wage-incentive systems, to minimize investment or maintenance costs of production equipment—in essence, convergent pressures of departmental budgetary performance systems—have made production quantity more important than production quality, and opportunity costs of a small percentage of quality defects were considered to be tolerable. Because perfect quality was considered to be practically an impossible goal, extra efforts and expenses to attain that goal were considered impractical or too costly. However, by the mid–1980s U.S. manufacturers became aware that their loss of competitiveness had been far more costly and had been caused by their neglect of work for the quality goal of zero defects.[5]

Quality-precision capabilities of production processes must be equal to or greater than those specified by product designed tolerances. Thus a unit produced is pronounced defective, because the measurement of its quality characteristic is outside the tolerance dimensions specified by the product design, and the production process should be immediately stopped to avoid production of more defective units. Statistical, random sampling of quality measurements is used to ascertain whether or not the process quality remains under control, i.e., that its range of variation is smaller than the range of variation permitted by the design specification. Those measurements of process-quality variations also enable planners and controllers of quality assurance to decide whether random samples or 100 percent inspection of all units is necessary to ensure the achievement of zero defects. Trends in process-quality measurements (e.g., means and variances of samples) also indicate the frequencies and methods for process maintenance and the need and time for investment in equipment replacement. Accordingly, Japanese manufacturers have effectively used 100 percent process-quality measurements to achieve goals of zero defects and statistical sampling records of those measurements for managing quality improvements.[6] Fortunately, by 1989 there was growing evidence that American manufacturers were reforming their management and improving their quality, not by inspecting quality into their products, but by using quality measurements as key indicators of immediate and long-term means for sustaining and improving their productivity and competitiveness.

PERSPECTIVES ON COMPUTERIZED MANAGEMENT OF CORPORATE COMPETITIVENESS

At this point, some readers might wonder why management science techniques and computers have been briefly cited but have not been expounded as the principal means for reviving U.S. manufacturing competitiveness. This is understandable, in light of the reviews of published research on manufacturing operations in academic and professional association journals. Most of those articles proclaim the effectiveness or efficiencies attainable by applying such techniques as MRP, artificial intelligence, mathematical (integer or operational) network programming, flexible automation, digital queuing systems simulation, multiplant production and inventory planning and control systems. Expositions of their logic and examples of their applications are both compelling and deserving of consideration.

However, I trust readers may also have realized that my proposals for manufacturers' revival are expounded more in generalized, humanistic terms than specialized, technocratic terms. Thus the purpose of the managers of manufacturing firms is to improve the product quality and increase the productive interdependency of more people, institutions and societies rather than to maximize profits. And the focus on the opportunity for quality improvements and earlier delivery to customers should be determined primarily via corporatewide consensus of priority choices *after* alternative opportunities have been considered. It is my contention that U.S. manufacturers have declined because they have "scientized" the management of their competitiveness. Computerized management talents, concepts and techniques have been acquired, organized, adopted and applied wherever feasible, without sufficient regard for their contributions to holistic needs or corporate priorities, goals and processes. As pointed out by David Halberstam in his book *The Reckoning*, computerized knowledge became power for bean counter financial managers to overrule car men concerned with the quality of the products and processes of the Ford Motor Company. In general, it seems reasonable to suggest that American manufacturers may have become scientized and lost their competitiveness, ironically, because their history and indulgences with organized proliferations of science have been longer and more extensive than those of their competitors or other industrial firms. People of U.S. manufacturing firms seem to have worked to serve the power and numbers (i.e., quantified value) of science, technology and finance, more than to manage their firms' product qualities and productivity to serve more people of society at large.

F. W. Taylor and Frank and Lillian Gilbreth originated and applied the scientific management of work processes in the early 1900s. In other words, they developed the technology and economics of micromotion time elements comprising human and material energy systems for manufacturing. Until computers, those systems were essentially controlled by and for people (managers, union and workers), notwithstanding popular observations by satirists or humorists such as Charlie Chaplin. However, after computers became available, whole networks of production lines were designed, measured and controlled via computerized information systems. Management became more technocratic and dehumanized, with power much more centralized, especially that of the financial managers responsible for measuring and controlling the flow and inventory of capital.

This is certainly not intended to be an indictment of the concepts or organizations of computerized management science by manufacturers. Rather my purpose is to suggest briefly: First that computerized management science applications may have been sponsored so profusely so as to have confused manufacturers' purposes, means and measures of achievement, and ironically to have caused their decline in competitiveness. Second, that evaluation of computerized management sciences for restoring corporate competitiveness should (indeed, probably must) be made case by case. It is for the CEO and the financial, technical and operating managers of each manufacturer to restructure, select and apply democratically and holistically computerized management systems to fulfill their priority needs for quality improvement and faster delivery for customers. What, where and how to apply computerized management science systems are issues for *democratic* (humanistic, not technocratic) decisions, therefore, intrinsic with each firm, case by case.

THE MANUFACTURING PROGRESS-EXPERIENCE CURVE

A very useful (noncomputerized) concept for managing corporate productivity growth is the manufacturing progress-experience curve, or the mathematical equation shown in figure 2. The logarithmic form of the curve is perhaps easier and more practical to use. The curve and the formula represent a manufacturer's plan for progress in managing productivity growth. Proper management of experiences according to the plan should mean a decrease in incremental efforts per unit as the number of units produced and sold to customers has been increased. Such a curve could be useful as a model or path for corporate growth in competitiveness, profitability or productivity if corporate experiences are planned and controlled effectively and accordingly.

The corporate progress-experience curve has a long history of effective applications by U.S. manufacturers. In 1938 Dr. Theodore Wright published the results of his research of empirical data on experiences with productivity of U.S. air-frame manufacturers. His findings, consistent for several manufacturers, indicated that as the cumulative number of air frames produced was doubled, expenditures of direct labor (hours or dollars) per unit were reduced by 20 percent. In other words, he called this

Figure 2
Manufacturing Progress-Experience Curve and Logarithm

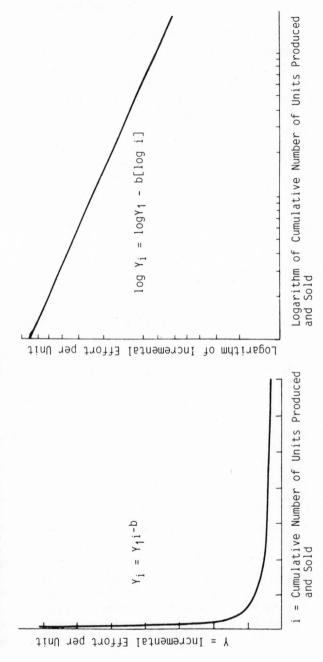

a corporate progress-experience rate of 80 percent.[7] Because this phenomenon is directly analogous with patterns of human learning experiences—manifestations observed, reported and used by psychologists, physiologists and learning therapists—it is also called the "corporate learning curve." During World War II, Wright was an official of the U.S. War Production Board and used the corporate learning curve effectively to ascertain and manage the human resources required for the growth of the U.S. aircraft industry. Since then, the curve has been used to assess experiences and strategies for corporate competition, for example, by the Boston Consulting Group, for its clients. The underlying precept relevant to U.S. manufacturers' revival is that corporate productivity growth and quality improvements are managed effectively according to such learning curves.

The curve is effective, used as projection of the future progress path to guide management of changes, i.e., improvements in qualities and productivity, which, of course, should improve corporate competitiveness. Experiences (i.e., incremental efforts and corporate output) are then measured and plotted continuously, to reveal evolutionary, i.e., short-term and long-term, comparison of corporate plans with corporate experiences.

Alternative measurements of corporate incremental efforts per unit include direct costs (direct materials plus direct labor expenses) per unit, direct labor expenses per unit and direct labor hours per unit. Cost or monetary dimensions are satisfactory and useful. But high U.S. inflation or volatile U.S.-foreign currency exchange rates might complicate their use as measurements of corporate progress and experiences during extended time periods. Therefore, direct labor hours per unit provide a more reliable measurement. It should be understood, however, that corporate incremental efforts are reduced and productivity growth occurs as results of *interdependent* efforts by all concerned: managers, technical staff and employees, classed by cost accountants as direct and indirect workers in supplier firms as well as the manufacturer's firm.

Use of the corporate progress-experience curve requires judgments of forecasts of past experiences and imagination, or creative expectations, about future experiences as is true of all management concepts and planning techniques. Thus for a family of products, the manufacturer can examine and plot the curve of recent historical data on the firm's own cumulative production output and associated, incremental input efforts. Then this empirical progress-rate parameter can be modified according to considerations of, and expectations from, current projects for quality and productivity improvements now in progress. Also comparable historical data, measuring experiences of other manufacturers and compiled by professional, trade or industrial associations, might be useful, especially if those data are known to pertain essentially to the same technologies of products and processes as those used by the manufacturer. These data would indicate desired or necessary changes from the firm's own, past experiences in order for its future progress to sustain its market position or to overtake that of its competitor(s).

The adoption of entirely new technology for a family of products, or their processing, may constitute a change so revolutionary as to be considered a precedent for entirely new curves for managing progress and experiences. Or they may be evolutionary changes manifested as discontinuities by the old, ongoing corporate progress-experience curve. However, progress-experience curves are useful because they facilitate quick, continuous comparisons of paths planned for progress and achieved by experiences as they accumulate, unit-by-unit produced. They can be used effectively in negotiations with suppliers to synchronize the suppliers' plans and progress with those of the manufacturer's efforts to improve competitiveness. Moreover, manufacturing progress-experience curves are valid, reliable, simple and holistic so that all rank-and-file employees as well as managers and technical specialists understand and are probably willing to perform and, perhaps, to be rewarded according to those curves.

ACQUISITION AND DEVELOPMENT OF HUMAN RESOURCES

We now consider closing a circle of proposals and completing our theme for U.S. manufacturers' revival, all based on human resources management. Initial recommendations were for CEOs and their organizations to treat the public (i.e., potential customers, consumer activists, environmentalists and business journalists) more as human resources for intelligence about quality improvements and funds (public or private) for those improvements and less as adversaries to be avoided or discredited, or subjects to be influenced or lobbied. The second group of proposals were for a more democratic, corporatewide focus of specialized talents for planning and executing improvements in quality and productivity and less technocratic, sequential concentrations of those talents. These recommendations are likely to be effective, if manufacturers change their policies and practices in acquiring and developing the firm's human resources per se. All employees (like customers, shareholders, suppliers, government bureaucrats and the general public) have a heavy stake in manufacturers' processes for financing, planning and executing quality and productivity improvements.

If U.S. manufacturers are to revive their roles as leading institutions for expanding the power and markets for industrial economic and political interdependence, then they should reform their human resources management to close the gaps between their economic doctrines for growth via economies of consistency and scale and growth via economies of more rapid technical/industrial change.

Generally, U.S. manufacturers have for too long persisted with rigidities of human resources management. Such persistence stems from their preoccupations with growth in mass-production capabilities and economies of scale. American manufacturers attained their preeminence as global competitors via such preoccupations during 1940–65, while the Japanese and the European manufacturers suffered and recovered from the damages of World War II.

Since the mid–1960s, manufacturers' growth has been influenced increasingly by internationalization of their markets, and by much more rapid exploitations of science and technology. International markets demanded product-quality variations to suit national cultures or laws of industrial/economic performance accountability. Nuclear physics and chemistry quickly became wellsprings for the new technologies of energy, materials and information. In turn, these technologies provoked more rapid changes in the qualities of products and processes. Thus orga-

nization and management of U.S. manufacturers' human resources need restructuring for more flexibility. Corporate growth
via economies of change is a requirement of corporate competitiveness as important as corporate growth via economies of
scale.

Credentials for Management

Greater flexibility of organizations and management means
more democracy, less bureaucracy and fewer powers of hierarchy. The president of Ford Motor Company noted the contrast
between five levels of rank between the lowest paid employees
and the highest paid executive of a Toyota division and eleven
levels of rank in Ford's Escort division, a direct competitor.[8] This
contrast stems from the rigid, class distinctions between U.S.
managers and workers and from the presumptions of adversarial
roles and practice of adversarial relations between managers and
labor unions in U.S. firms.

Academic degrees are practically exclusive credentials for admission to the ranks and practice of U.S. manufacturing management. If U.S. manufacturers would acknowledge and adopt
credentials of experience as well as credentials of academic curricula, then their processes for democratic, participatory management of quality and productivity improvements would
become more effective. The levels, or ranks, or hierarchy
would be reduced, and there would be fewer inhibitions and
delays in genuine discussions and consensus because gaps of
hierarchical status would be eliminated. By providing for and
recognizing values of their employees' experiential accomplishments (i.e., productivity), U.S. manufacturers would contribute substantially to increase the effectiveness and relevance of
academic education by U.S. colleges and universities for managers, engineers, accountants, economists, etc. This is not a
proposal for manufacturers necessarily to boost their philanthropic support for higher education, but to boost their effectiveness in managing the economies of industrial change via
restructuring the management of their human resources. U.S.
manufacturers could provide more challenging practical experiences as credentials for students, while universities would

provide more rigorous, relevant academic curricula as credentials for managers. Faculty could take leaves to practice as managers or engineers or scientists at industrial firms, while the latter could take leaves to practice as educators, researchers or teachers at universities. Problems of conflict could arise between the proprietary interests of manufacturers and the academic freedom of knowledge upheld by universities. But precedents for controlling those problems effectively can be taken from extensive experiences in joint research efforts by industrial firms and universities. The dual credentials of experiences by manufacturing employees and academic degrees by university graduates would serve to diffuse the differences of status between faculty and students and between managers and workers and to close the gaps of hierarchy in their relations. Consequently, human resources of both manufacturers and industrial/professional programs of universities would be improved.

Relatedly, by closing the gaps of status between managers and workers, manufacturers could more easily shift from adversarial to more cooperative positions in their relations with unions, all toward the end of more democratic, participative and effective management of their competitiveness. Vying with each other over working conditions has meant that for too long, American managers and unions have ignored or sacrificed their firm's competitive standing. However, there has been growing evidence during recent years that union-management cooperation is a top priority requirement for U.S. manufacturers' survival and growth, whether by sharing corporate risks and costs of quality improvement and productivity growth or by joining together in political efforts to persuade the federal government to try to enact improvements in foreign or domestic market conditions for their firm and industry. By and large, unions and managers of foreign manufacturers have been more cooperative and less adversarial, while wages, working conditions and benefits for health, housing, dependents, job security and retirement pensions have been raised to levels nearly comparable with (or for Japanese and Western European firms, exceeding) those of American manufacturers. More genuine, equitable union-management cooperation is a prerequisite for smarter (not harder) work and progress toward improving corporate competitiveness.

If U.S. manufacturers recognize and reward the human credentials of corporate experiences (along with those of academic curricula) and adopt a cooperative, instead of adversarial, attitude in their relations with unions, then they will restore the corporate democracy and flexibility needed for achieving both economies of scale and economies of change.

Human power and relations and interdependencies have to be organized (i.e., classified and ranked) so that institutions are manageable and kinds and degrees of authority and responsibility are clearly understood. But when classes of bureaucratic separations grow too strong or ranks of management hierarchy become too numerous, corporate management impedes (instead of enhances) change and progress. The fundamental principles of democratic self-governance have been violated or repressed. It is not scientifically possible to specify and control the conditions of organizations and management so that order, consistency and efficiency of social class, bureaucracies and hierarchies always enhance and never stultify human progress. Those conditions have to be created pragmatically. (Whether organizations and management are the subjects and practices of the sciences or arts and humanities is a recent issue of controversy by management educators, most notably those of Yale University and its school of organization and management.)[9] But it is nonetheless logical to recommend that more democratic (less autocratic or technocratic) relations among American managers, workers and unions would enhance quality improvements and productivity growth of U.S. manufacturers. By treating workers' contributions equally with students' academic degrees as credentials for promotion, appointment or admission to practice as managers, U.S. managers would democratize and improve not only the values of their human resources and corporate performance but those of the professional schools, such as management, engineering and applied sciences, at American universities.

Along with the participatory management of projects for quality improvements and productivity growth, these initiatives would very likely affect further reductions desired in the levels of corporate hierarchy and in the rigidities and the gaps among corporate bureaucracies—in short, a U.S. version of *glasnost* and *perestroika* to improve American democratic management of economies of scale with economies of change!

Compensation for Management

Reforms of compensation schemes for managers and employees are consistent with the proposals for more democracy, self-determination and flexibility about acquiring, developing and utilizing human resources. Morale, productivity growth, innovative capabilities and competitiveness of U.S. manufacturers have declined, not only because of disintegration by their managers of finance from their managers of operations, or because of widening gaps among their hierarchies and bureaucracies. Gaps of inequities in compensation have also been a major cause.

In 1960, the annual remuneration received by a typical CEO of a large U.S. manufacturing firm was an average of 41 times the average pay received by the factory worker. In 1988, the CEO's remuneration had jumped to 93 times that of the U.S. factory worker.[10] This dramatic change occurred while U.S. manufacturers' competitiveness declined. Surely it reflects blatant ignorance of concerns for *management by example* (not "management by objectives"). If compensation for top, active corporate executives continues to grow conspicuously above and beyond the ballpark of corporate compensation for middle managers and workers, then work teams, quality circles, union-management cooperation and democratic-participatory management are probably foredoomed to failure. Corporate employees' rewards should be suitable not only to their hierarchical positions or their performance contributions, but perhaps most important, to the *moral integrity* of the human effort committed to the growth in corporate profits, productivity, economies of scale or economies of change. Just as human corporate efforts must be planned, measured and controlled via processes suitable for all corporate stakeholders, so too, should corporate compensation for those efforts.

Because all human resources should be considered and utilized as management capabilities, it follows logically (in principle, even though not always rigorously in practice) that manufacturers should plan and execute one, single corporate compensation scheme for all (CEO, top functional or division executives, middle managers, first-line supervisors and employees classed as direct and indirect labor). It is not logical in this discussion to propose detailed contents of such schemes. Each must be designed and utilized, pragmatically and, preferably, democratically, according to measures of corporate risks and opportunities defined by each manufacturer. Generally, however, the compensation scheme should indicate the terms of corporate bonuses, contingent on corporate profits earned.

Preferably, wage incentives or individual, group or departmental production piece-rate compensation plans should be abandoned. They are antithetical to the holistical corporate goals of quality improvements and productivity growth for customers (i.e., to increase corporate competitiveness). Some firms have adopted compensation schemes providing "two-tiered" salaries, lower for newly hired employees and higher for long-tenured staff, although they are both performing the same duties. Two-tiered salaries are not recommended because of their demoralizing effects of permanent gaps in the salaries of employees with the same jobs.

CONCLUSION

Starting from the ruins of World War II, Japanese and Western European manufacturers demonstrated, once again, the fundamental truths about economic growth processes. Making more and better products for more people precedes delivering more services or making more money. Manufacturers' products enable more people, worldwide, to live, work and serve more productively and invest more profitably together. It follows that U.S. manufacturers would improve their competitiveness by acting more as institutions dedicated to production and less to financing or services.

Politically, or economically, people freely determine the value of products, i.e., the quality, availability and price in relation to those of their (peoples') other necessities. Manufacturers' democratic relations with people (i.e., corporate stakeholders) are more important than the technocratic relations among concepts or conventions for accounting and measuring economic or industrial progress, or values of products, because the morale, self-governance and mutual commitments of stakeholders determine corporate growth. Corporate stakeholders alone provide assurance that the value of the corporate whole exceeds the sum of its parts.

Scientific and quantitative analyses and measurements of corporate components of processes are necessary and useful for the sake of the firm as a whole. Teamwork by suppliers, managers, workers and customers makes those processes and measurements relate *synergistically* as a corporate whole. It is only because of the necessities and conventions of accountability, universal (political or economic) understanding or analytical (technical or economic) convenience that corporate process measurements are related *additively as a mathematical whole* (or corporate model), even though for those process measurements to be truly additive they must be *mutually independent* (which, of course, they are not).

The manufacturing firm will survive and grow so long as its stakeholders act as if its corporate whole is greater than the sum of its individualistic independent capabilities. This is why manufacturing firms are the primary institutions for growth in global interdependence wrought by industrial civilization. But if manufacturing executives act as if corporate process measurements are more important than (or even indicate the status of) corporate morale and democratic processes for self-governance, then, ironically, their firm's competitiveness, productivity and profitability are put at risk. As is true in competitive sports, the game of corporate growth in global market competitiveness cannot be played strictly according to the rules for keeping score or measuring performance. Instead, manufacturers must manage to compete via quality improvements and teamwork that may require improvements in corporate measurements and changes in corporate accountability. The validity of this conclusion has become more apparent from industrial stakeholders' worldwide concerns about qualities and availability of manufacturers' products and their threats to human and ecological health and safety; threats of nuclear accidents or holocaust, armed terrorism, military repressions or insurgencies; and threats of despoliation of the earth's nonrenewable resources required for sustaining the lives of growing populations.

NOTES

1. James Fallows, *More Like Us: Making America Great Again* (Boston: Houghton Mifflin, 1989).
2. W. Edwards Deming, an American consultant on managing the product and process quality of Japanese manufacturers for decades following World War II, was so appreciated for his contributions that the Japanese endowed and rewarded an annual nationally esteemed prize for efforts continued in his name.
3. Kenneth A. Wantuck, corporate director of materials management for Bendix Corporation, wrote "The ABC's of Japanese Productivity," *Production & Inventory Management Review* (September 1981): 22–28.
4. E. Goldratt, CEO of Creative Output, Inc., consultants and developers of OPT, in lectures to U.S. professors of operations management, University of Arizona, June 24–27, 1986.
5. For example, see Gregory L. Miles, "Forging the New Bethlehem Steel Co.," *Business Week* (June 6, 1989): 106–108.
6. Dr. Shigeo Shingo, consultant in quality and president of the Institute of Japanese Management Improvements, in a lecture presented at the University of Massachusetts at Amherst, May 10, 1989.
7. T. P. Wright, vice president of Curtis Wright, as reported by R. Conway and A. Schultz, "The Manufacturing Progress Function," *Journal of Industrial Engineering* (January–February 1959).
8. Harry B. Ellis, "More Lessons from Japan," *Christian Science Monitor*, December 15, 1980, p. 1.
9. James R. Norman, "Days of Rage at Yale B-School," *Business Week*, December 12, 1988, p. 36.
10. Dean Foust and Monica Roman, "Is the Boss Getting Paid Too Much?" *Business Week* (May 1, 1989): 46–48.

5

U.S. Manufacturers' Revival: Reform by the U.S. Government

Earlier we pointed out that U.S. manufacturers have declined since 1965 because of the U.S. government's security strategy for global military deterrence and containment of Soviet Marxist-Leninist expansion; its monetary policies, first for preserving the $35 per ounce gold commitment, then abandoning that commitment and devaluing the dollar in exchange for the Japanese yen and German deutsche mark; and its financial policies for safeguarding loan repayments by Latin American countries. We also noted that, paradoxically, the U.S. government has executed de facto a national industrial policy for sustaining a global military/industrial hegemony, while complaining increasingly about national industrial policies of allied governments for acquiring advanced technology and supporting global growth of their manufacturers of consumer/industrial products.

At the time of this writing (mid–1989), there were growing indications that the U.S.-Soviet cold war was ending as well as the obsolescent, national security requirements for U.S. global military deterrence capabilities sustained by U.S. manufacturers—for example, the U.S.-Soviet agreement to abolish intermediate-range nuclear weapons and the negotiations for significant reductions in strategic nuclear weapons and conventional weapons deployed with NATO forces in Europe. But these indications had not raised prospects, much less prompted enactments, of significant cuts in U.S. weapons procurement programs. Washington leaders refused to execute major reductions, because of the strong apprehension about trust and geopolitical/ military power and security of Soviet President Mikhail Gorbachev and because of their equally strong fears of losing their own political power and security if they inflicted U.S. weapons manufacturers with heavy losses of markets, profits, jobs and income.

Still, concerns persisted about federal deficits, trade deficits, loan repayments by Latin American countries and U.S. manufacturers' competitiveness. The U.S. Defense Advanced Research Project Agency (DARPA) funded a $200 million project to develop technology for high-definition television (HDTV), thus enabling U.S. firms to compete with Japanese manufacturers in large, global markets expected for HDTV equipment. And congressional leaders voiced strong apprehensions about threats to U.S. aircraft manufacturers' competitiveness from the U.S.–Japanese government agreement to cooperate in a program to develop an advanced tactical fighter aircraft (FSX), based substantially on U.S. technology of F–16 aircraft manufactured by General Dynamics Corporation.

Thus Washington leaders acted as if electronic and aircraft manufacturers' technologies were important as requirements for U.S. national security. But they appeared unaware of practical ways to shift priorities, programs and funding by the U.S. government from military/industrial to civil/industrial security and growth in foreign and domestic security affairs of American people and their institutions. And they had not linked needs and means for increasing manufacturers' competitiveness with needs and means for changing national security strategies of the U.S. government.

U.S.-ALLIED MILITARY/INDUSTRIAL COOPERATION

As suggested in chapter 3, Washington leaders should acknowledge their U.S. national policies for military/industrial *in-*

dependence and adverse effects of their conflict with U.S. national policies to foster free and fair trade and civil/industrial *interdependence* with Western democratic and industrializing nations. If U.S. manufacturers are to restore their competitive capabilities effectively, then the U.S. government should initiate programs for U.S.-allied military/industrial cooperation in order to eliminate this policy conflict.

U.S. global power stems mostly from U.S. manufacturing capabilities. During and since World War II, that power was manifested chiefly by U.S. military/industrial growth. More recently, in addition to *glasnost*, *perestroika* and Soviet global military concessions, changes in the relations with allies and in U.S. domestic security requirements clearly indicate opportunities to shift U.S. priorities from military/industrial growth to civil/industrial growth. This transformation of national industrial policies can be accomplished via U.S. initiatives for military/industrial and civil/industrial cooperation with allied nations of NATO, Japan and Australia.

To sustain *remaining* requirements for their military security the U.S. should initiate partnerships for allied governments to cooperate in funding and procurement, while arms manufacturers would form contractors' consortia, merge interests or compete in developing and producing common, standard, conventional weapons. The formation and execution of U.S.-allied cooperative arms programs would enhance the solidarity of Western democracies, and this would probably accelerate progress in East-West negotiations for military reductions in Europe. Still, mutual requirements for Western security from military forces of the Middle East, Africa, Asia and Latin America would remain sufficient reasons for U.S.-allied cooperation. And advantages of acquiring more effective, conventional weapons for substantially lower costs would make it desirable for the U.S. and Western allies to launch cooperative arms-procurement programs.

The roles of partner governments and manufacturers would be determined essentially in accordance with partner governments' agreement of their proportionate shares of total funds or the total number of weapons involved in their initial procurement. Subsequent procurement actions might occur, because of additional needs of partner governments. They would form a weapon program organization, staffed appropriately by representatives of their ministries of defense, military services, finance and accounting or procurement contract administrations. They would negotiate a prime contract specifying uniform terms of technical, financial and legal accountability and performance, including procedures for raising and adjudicating contract disputes by partner governments, the prime contractor and all associate or subcontractors engaged in the program.

U.S. initiatives for such cooperation would very likely elicit positive response by allied governments for several reasons. Precedents for such cooperation exist in Europe, where cost-effective programs were conducted to produce NATO Hawk missiles and NATO Starfighter aircraft and, more recently, F–16 tactical aircraft; the United States and Japan have cooperated in producing P–3V patrol aircraft, Starfighter aircraft and the advanced tactical fighter aircraft (FSX) program launched in 1989. Moreover, arms/industrial cooperative programs enable partner nations to develop and use high technology and to increase employment, sales and exports by the manufacturing firms, while providing the most effective weapons at minimum costs for production, operation and maintenance. Also, U.S.-allied cooperation would enable Western governments to avoid redundant, costly investments in several development and production programs for different weapons intended for the same military missions and to avoid the pressure to compete with each other for arms exports to other governments, to spread the burden of weapons development and production cost among a larger number of governments. As noted, in the past such pressures have expanded and intensified the East-West arms race, destabilized political and economic conditions and thus curtailed or destroyed opportunities to develop civil/industrial trade and political relations with nonaligned nations. (Those latter relations are bonds of Western nonaligned interdependence, which are far more effective as deterrents of Fascist or Marxist expansion than the bonds established as results of exports of Western weapons.) Finally, U.S.-allied arms/industrial cooperation would avert the pressure for political, economic and industrial protectionism, which, during recent years, have seriously strained the bonds of Western interdependence and jeopardized expansion and growth of the common markets required by Western manufacturers. The United States has accrued large and serious deficits. But it is still the "critical mass market" for investment, production and income opportunities and for exercising free enterprise, political and economic systems of each and every Western nation. Allied governments of NATO, Japan and Australia would, therefore, be likely to respond favorably, to U.S. invitations of partnerships in funding and procurement of conventional weapons.

For the United States, arms/industrial cooperation with allied governments would enable much larger, more rapid and, yet, politically viable reductions in federal expenditures. The United States and its NATO allies would remain united so that negotiations for arms reduction with the Soviets could proceed more expeditiously, with minimum strain or risk of breach in Western allies' relations. Common, standard weapons would increase NATO's conventional military effectiveness by 50 percent, so that the United States, the U.K. and France might renounce their longstanding threat of first use of tactical nuclear weapons against the invasion by Warsaw Pact conventional forces. Thus the United States might abandon its plans to replace the Lance, short-range nuclear weapons and its efforts to reinterpret its ABM Treaty with the Soviets and to deploy "Star Wars" weapons, which have obstructed negotiations and agreement with the Soviets for significant reductions of strategic nuclear weapons. Relations among the European nations, which are most threatened by theater nuclear war, could continue to improve, and perhaps the iron curtain and Berlin Wall could be torn down, physically and ideologically. Cuts in Washington's federal deficit would appeal to European allies who, in the past, expressed concerns that those deficits and high U.S. interest payments caused scarce capital funds to flow from their countries to the United States.

U.S. domestic political conditions would also be improved. Arms/industrial cooperation with allies would mean that the U.S. Army, Navy and Air Force would have greater difficulties competing with each other by procuring different weapons from different contractors—intended to perform the same military missions. Relatedly, U.S.-allied arms/industrial cooperation would probably terminate political, economic and industrial pork barrel arrangements between the Pentagon and powerful congressmen and senators and reduce, if not eliminate, possibilities for procurement scandals arising from cozy, corrupt, conspiratorial deals by defense consultants, Pentagon procurement officials and U.S. weapons manufacturers.

Cooperative weapons programs would create a common Atlantic and Pacific defense market in which U.S. defense contractors would be free to compete, consort or merge interests with their counterpart firms of Western nations under their governments' uniform, equitable terms of accountability. These conditions would enhance their prospects for performance in common international markets for consumer/industrial products. The cooperative programs would probably provide U.S. defense firms with larger market, production and income opportunities than those likely to be provided by the Pentagon acting alone without partner governments and after the almost certain future U.S. cuts in defense expenditures.

Perhaps most important, cooperative arms programs could provide for more equitable sharing of the Western defense burden, even while total Western defense needs and costs are being reduced as the result of East-West arms-reduction agreements. For the United States this could mean reductions in annual defense expenditures of about $100 billion. The savings could then be used to finance three vital and growing security needs of Americans and Western allies: (1) to reduce the federal deficit and the burden of interest payments and cash outflow to foreign investors in U.S. Treasury bonds, notes, etc; (2) to finance programs to manufacture equipment and construct facilities badly needed in the United States for infrastructure improvements of education, mass transportation, water resources, housing, health services, energy conservation and environmental pollution controls, public safety and satellite weather information-control systems; and (3) to finance a U.S. government policy for promoting U.S. manufacturers' export trade and global competitiveness, via a Marshall Plan revival and cooperative civil/industrial development programs with nonaligned nations.

In essence, this proposal is for Washington leaders to change

U.S. national security strategies, products and roles of U.S. manufacturers by shifting its national industrial policy (de facto) from that of national military/industrial independence to dual policies for military and civil/industrial interdependence with Western democracies, nonaligned Third World nations and, perhaps eventually, Soviet bloc nations. As this shift of national industrial policy is executed, there would be a steady diminution of the domestic political and financial roles of the national security establishment bureaucrats (CIA, National Security Council, national security staff of the White House, Pentagon, FBI, expert think tank consultants and Pentagon procurement officials), and in the foreign, geopolitical roles of the officers and enlisted personnel of the U.S. military. But the decline in these roles would be offset by an increase in the roles of U.S. manufacturers at home and abroad. The significance of the advantages from such offset is most important because the free, competitive, open democratic, market economic accountability and productive effects of their management of U.S. manufacturing operations (in contrast with military operations) would enhance their own competitiveness, and strengthen American security via expanding the bonds of productive, civil/industrial interdependence on trade, jobs, products and services shared by Americans with the peoples of allied and Third World nations. U.S. manufacturing personnel would become peacemaking activists or catalysts, gradually replacing peacekeeping capabilities no longer required of U.S. military personnel.

Nearly 50 years of experience with hot and cold wars, military power for deterrence, and their requisite politics of secrecy, fear, distrust and cynicism may have preconditioned Washington leaders to oppose alternative strategies for national security. Their declarations and programs for wars against crime, drugs, poverty and intolerance of minority groups have demonstrated their decades-old psychopolitical preferences to fight or deter (instead of avoid or eliminate) threats to social security. So at first these proposed changes in U.S. national/industrial security policies may seem too idealistic and impractical for serious consideration by Washington officials. However, the United States is a 200-year-old, constitutional democracy, of which the majority of its citizens (3 to 1) want the government to reduce its global hegemony for wars. Significant numbers of Americans, including politicians, scientists, lawyers, educators. physicians, clergymen, women's organizations and retired officers and enlisted military personnel, have invested in movements for converting American military/industrial capabilities to fulfill the more urgently required civil/industrial and economic purposes of peaceful and productive interdependence. And Washington's leaders seem to have been discredited or subordinated by President Gorbachev's initiatives to abandon direct military confrontations with the United States in Europe and indirect surrogate confrontations in Asia, Africa and Latin America as well as by counterpart leaders of allied nations (notably, West Germany and South Korea), who have grown less supportive of U.S. military/industrial growth and deployment of more destructive weapons in their countries.

As indicated, for Western democracies, the security opportunities far exceed the security risks from U.S. efforts to cooperate with allied governments in funding and procurement of conventional weapons, in reducing (if not eliminating) exports of those weapons to nonaligned Third World nations, in reviving a Marshall Plan for strengthening civil/industrial trade and closing political and economic gaps between Western democracies and Third World nations. Western security from military forces for Soviet Marxist-Leninist expansion in European or Asian Rim countries would be sustained and allied military burdens balanced, then reduced, as East-West nuclear and conventional arms reductions were executed and verified. The Marshall Plan revival would enhance Western security from threats of political, ideological and terrorist forces for Marxist (Soviet or Chinese) expansion in South Asia, Africa and Latin America, because the power of Marxism would be overcome by the civil democratic power of stakeholders in Western and nonaligned governments; manufacturing firms; and agricultural, educational, financial and service institutions working together in each program. (After all, the essential issues of the ideological conflict between Marxist, Leninist socialist and democratic, free enterprise systems are those of politics and economics and the free exercise of power by individual stakeholders of government and industry. The

Western allies' Marshall Plan with Third World nations would confront and resolve those issues, most likely on Western terms, with little or no military force needed!)

PROBLEMS AND PRECEDENTS FROM EXPERIENCES WITH U.S.-ALLIED ARMS/ INDUSTRIAL COOPERATION

To execute a U.S. policy for military/industrial cooperation effectively is to overcome the probable resistance to change stemming from tradition or myths about the power of national sovereignty. Throughout all of history, the power of military forces has been the ultimate or divine right of kings or the sovereign power of national government. Beliefs in national sovereignty remain strong, despite the fact that the U.S. and Western allied governments strengthened their security and interdependence in civil/industrial and economic affairs and sustained their military alliances. Yet, paradoxically, U.S.-allied military/industrial cooperative programs may be resisted by some government officials on the grounds that those programs would reduce the sovereign power of their government to act as exclusive patron, director or customer of its national arms industry, and consequently, as commander of its armed forces. It is helpful to anticipate such resistance so there are more careful plans and patient, pragmatic efforts to launch the U.S. policy for military/ industrial interdependence with democratic governments of the North Atlantic and Pacific areas. The French are rather widely perceived as zealous protectors of the power of their national sovereignty, vis-à-vis those of NATO. Yet the French effectively sustained their key responsibility for systems engineering and management of the U.S.-NATO Hawk Cooperative Production Program, even after President Charles de Gaulle ordered NATO headquarters to be moved from Paris and the French military forces to withdraw from NATO-integrated commands.[1]

There are other lessons from the experience with U.S.-allied military/industrial cooperative programs launched by the Eisenhower administration and executed during the early 1960s. These lessons might be useful if the policy for U.S.-allied military/industrial interdependence is revived and executed during the 1990s.

On their formal execution and ratification of the agreement to cooperate, partner governments should remain bound and committed for the duration of the cooperative development and production of the weapons acquired by their program. Programs are organized and staffed by both governments and contractors, and their offices are located respectively, according to shares of total estimated expenditures and total number of weapons to be procured by partner governments. Although a partner government might decide to increase its share of the total procurement, and thereby extend the duration of the program, a reduction or cancellation of its initial agreement and obligations should be avoided. If such a reduction or cancellation is unavoidable, then that partner government should agree to pay a fee to cover the costs to remaining partner governments of changes and delays in plans and organizations for the program. Startup and structural matters of weapon-system programs, organizations, policies and procedures of governments and manufacturers' consortia are costly, time-consuming and difficult (political, economic, technical and legal) issues. They ought to be faced and resolved once, at the outset of the program, so that plans and operations are manageable. Partner governments' agreements for military/industrial cooperation should not be capricious, because they become bonds of interdependent livelihood among scientists, engineers, managers, unions, workers, military officers and enlisted personnel—all stakeholders affected concretely by such agreement.

Another lesson is that programs may serve to fulfill the different purposes of partner governments, for example, to acquire the best weapons possible from manufacturers located in any Western allied nation (not those located only in nations of partner governments), because the lowest price and shortest delivery time are the highest priorities. Another example would be to acquire the best weapons possible from manufacturers operating existing factories in partner-nations, because avoidance of deficits in international trade of currency exchange is the highest priority concern. Or the program may try to obtain the best weapons possible from manufacturers willing to invest and construct new factory production capabilities in a region of partners' nations, because industrial/economic development is the highest priority concern. In the course of their discussions to determine whether or not to form partnerships, governments should make known their respective priorities and purposes to be accomplished before they agree to launch the program. They might invite participation by competing prime contractors who would be asked to submit proposals for different consortia of associate and subcontractors to be formed in response, according to the different purposes and priorities of the governments. Of course, governments would pay for the costs of the different proposals and incur greater expenses and efforts to evaluate the proposals, select and combine the best features of the different proposals and negotiate accordingly with the prime contractor. However, those additional costs might be more than offset by the values of information and political and economic advantages afforded by the process of obtaining the alternative proposals from competing prime contractors. Manufacturers would become more directly and extensively involved with the decisions affecting all security purposes of government (military, political, economic and industrial), which, of course, directly and indirectly, affect their own priorities and purposes of growth (profits, productivity, competitiveness and product improvements). When manufacturers and governments focus holistically on their mutual concerns for security and progress, then democratic, free-enterprise systems of governments and industries are more likely to be most effective in accomplishing their missions of serving societies.

Proprietary interests, ownership and control of new technology developed by the program are also important concerns. Relevant laws of partner governments may be different and, therefore, cause problems in negotiating contracts with legally binding, uniform terms for partner governments and all contractors to work together in the weapons program. A suggested compromise of those differences would be for partner governments to confer rights and patent ownership to the contractor who originally developed the technology, but to retain their governmental rights to authorize other manufacturers to use the patented information without royalty fees in other weapons production programs. Thus because partner governments financed the development of the patent for the mutual purposes of their military security, logically and legally, they would retain the rights of further use of the patented technology for their military purposes. But the contractor owner of the patent would retain control of its uses for all other purposes (civil/industrial, public or private) so that the security and benefits of private, free enterprise, industrial/economic markets would be preserved and enhanced by U.S.-allied military/industrial cooperative weapons programs.

Along with the units of weapons' hardware ordered, each partner government should acquire a "technical data package" containing specifications for the design, manufacture, operations and maintenance of the weapon system. This package would enable each government to plan for improvements in the next generation of the weapon systems or to execute procurement of additional units of the present system, if the needs for those additional units arose after the initial acquisitions had been completed and the original production consortia of manufacturers had been dissolved. Acquiring the technical data packages would also enable partner governments to plan and maintain their national industrial policies, respectively, so that they would be more complementary than competitive. Thus governments' programs for military/industrial cooperation would enhance their international cooperation (and reduce their competition or protectionism) on matters of their national industrial policies for political and economic security. At the same time, those programs would enhance opportunities for manufacturers to compete, to act in consort or joint ventures or to merge interests in the common markets, which U.S.-allied cooperative weapons acquisition programs had helped to create.

Pursuant to acquisition of the technical data package, partner governments and manufacturers would, together, have to manage its development, because the development and production of conventional weapon systems require both governments and manufacturers to manage changes in technical qualities, delivery schedules and costs of the weapons produced and acquired. Each and every change affects a change in the technical, financial and legal terms of the contract for interdependence of the partner governments and the international consortia of contractors. Change management, or management of improvements in product quality or process productivity, is essential to manufacturing competitiveness. It is also a vital concern of U.S. manufacturers, because, in global markets during recent decades, change management by Japanese and Western European manufacturers has proved to be superior to change management by U.S. manufacturers.

For U.S.-allied cooperative weapons programs, U.S. Western European and Japanese manufacturers would spend years working together developing high-tech, conventional weapon systems. Thus those programs would afford significant opportunities for U.S. manufacturers to improve their management of changes. Historically, European and Japanese manufacturers have been more completely theoretical and analytical, i.e., more prudent, in managing technological improvements, because they have not had access to the basic resources of energy and materials as easily (i.e., as quickly or cheaply) as American manufacturers. Americans, traditionally, have resorted more to an experiential management of changes (i.e., "to bend metal or cut chips") and thus to exert less theoretical or analytical efforts in planning and controlling changes. This cultural difference between American and European or Japanese management of changes has been manifested by weapons technology development processes during the past 50 years. European theoretical physicists and chemists were most influential in nuclear weapons development (e.g., contributions by Albert Einstein, Niels Bohr and Enrico Fermi), and originators of radar, jet engines and missiles were European, not American, scientists and engineers. Moreover, in this age of computers, theoretical analytical methods of managing technical changes or product quality improvements are likely to be less costly and time-consuming than experiential methods. However, the point of emphasis here is that U.S.-allied cooperative weapons development and production programs would afford very significant opportunities for American technical experts and managers of both government agencies and manufacturing firms to engage intensively and extensively about issues and methods of change management with their Japanese and European counterparts. Direct results would very likely be lower costs, fewer delays in delivery and better-performing weapon systems. But perhaps more significant, indirect results would be the improvements in American capabilities for change management and manufacturing competitiveness in markets for consumer/industrial products.

For U.S. government officials there may be questions of timing and changes in industrial conditions for launching its policy for international cooperative programs. For examples: Should the U.S. government "go international" always and only during the earliest stage of development and never after production contracts and programs entirely with U.S. contractors had been launched? Or, should the U.S. government "internationalize" its funding and procurement of any or all planned and ongoing conventional weapons programs, whether or not its procurement contract commitments had already been made exclusively with U.S. contractors? Of course, allied, partner governments might also address their own complementary versions of these questions. To launch the U.S. policy for military/industrial cooperation with allied democracies may require change management by governments and manufacturers on a grand, unprecedented scale of enlightened, pragmatic, political and economic assessments of costs and benefits. Governments may have to pay for contract cancellations and delivery delays, and manufacturers may have to face international competitors and the risks of lost business, or contractors' consortia may have to be reorganized and the scope of their contracts for development or production changed for them to continue as participants in the U.S.-allied cooperative program. These costs and difficulties are real and would have to be pragmatically managed, program by program, by partner governments and contracting firms. But they are small when compared with the total long-term benefits from U.S.-allied military/industrial cooperation: minimized total burdens and maximized equities of U.S. and allied shares of Western security in all its dimensions (political, military, economic, industrial and social) in the future and, most important, the benefits from the reduction or elimination of those inequities people have suffered because their governments had failed to cooperate in a world of interdependence forged as an international security requirement by financial and industrial institutions, mostly manufacturing firms of Western democracies. In other words, industries have made Western democracies so interdependent that U.S. and allied governments' cooperative funding and procurement of common, conventional weapons have become a requirement as vital or urgent for them to manage as deterrent capabilities of their military forces for their national or mutual security.

Because their per capita GNP is approximately equal, it follows that equitable shares of Western defense burdens could be interpreted to mean that the United States, NATO, Japan and Australia spent about the same percentages of their respective GNP for defense. As noted earlier, U.S.-allied governments' cooperative weapons programs would provide the opportunities for sharing the defense burden, because allied industries would be able to compete and grow more efficiently in common international defense markets created by the programs. And common standard weapons produced by those programs would enable allies to reduce their total operating, maintenance and training costs. Calculations using the latest data on defense spending by Western democracies published by the U.S. Arms Control and Disarmament Agency, indicate that U.S.-allied military/industrial cooperative programs would enable the U.S. to reduce safely the Pentagon's annual budget by about $100 billion. And indications from more recent U.S.-Soviet arms negotiations and from U.S.-allied solidarity enhanced by those programs are that total U.S. defense expenditures could be reduced by substantially more than $100 billion per year. These savings are urgent requirements for Washington leaders to finance restoration of U.S. industrial and economic security.

A U.S. CIVIL/INDUSTRIAL UNIVERSITY COMPLEX, U.S. NATIONAL INDUSTRIAL POLICY: INFRASTRUCTURE SUPPORT AND APPROPRIATE TECHNOLOGY FOR MANUFACTURERS

Washington should reinvest those savings in federal deficit reductions and public infrastructure improvements, so that U.S. manufacturers can revive their competitiveness more effectively. In the United States and in nonaligned Third World countries, improvements are seriously needed in the public infrastructure-support systems for education, human and environmental health, housing, energy, transportation and agriculture. These improvements should be recognized as national industrial security requirements for U.S. manufacturers' processes and products to provide *economies of change and economies of scale* for more customers at home and abroad. In effect, this proposal is for Washington leaders to execute their own, noncontroversial version of a national industrial policy for the United States.

National industrial policy has been a controversial subject in the United States, because it is concerned with whether the U.S. government should exercise its authority in assigning priorities for different technologies and, accordingly, allocating national economic resources for civil/industrial growth. (Note that this is different from U.S. government's concerns about the qualities of U.S. public infrastructure-support systems for U.S. manufacturers.) Governments of Western Europe and Japan have exercised authority in industrial priorities and economic resource allocations since World War II, largely because of their stronger traditions of democratic socialism and their more severe limitations of industrial/economic resources compared with the United States. And their manufacturers have grown more productive and competitive compared with the record of U.S. manufacturers, since about 1965. Leaders of U.S. industry and government have correctly resisted the adoption of a U.S. national industrial policy for governmental priorities and economic resource allocations, because its execution, they allege, would create bureaucracies for national socialism and resistance to change required by industrial/economic growth. U.S. leaders have also declined to acknowledge that the Pentagon's management of U.S. arms procurements and exports has become equivalent to the execution of a U.S. national industrial policy de facto. They cite the small percentage of U.S. GNP affected by Pentagon procurements and exports, but they have ignored the significance of the leveraged effects the Pentagon has had on U.S. manufacturers, because of the top U.S. priorities and largest percentages of scarce funds and scientific and engineering talents allocated to security purposes of more destructive weapons for military deterrence. However, Washington's policies for public infrastructure improvements would improve U.S.

education, transportation and energy resources and enable U.S. manufacturers to manage their own improvements in product qualities and growth in productivity or competitiveness more effectively. Washington's investments to improve public infrastructure systems would be aimed at supporting U.S. manufacturers' conversion from products for military markets to products for civil markets. Those investments would very likely catalyze complementary investments by state, regional or community governments, because, of course, they are stakeholders in the stability and growth of employment, income and markets for U.S. manufacturers and the service industries that depend on factory production operations. The federal government could manage its investments so that nationwide public infrastructure improvements would be more equitable and would not exacerbate the U.S. regional gaps of industrial, economic and educational capabilities that have grown during recent decades to cause crime, poverty, drugs, illiteracy, etc. to be more concentrated in some communities or regions than in others. Of course, instead of secretly working with one bureaucracy—the Pentagon—Congress would work more openly and democratically with many different federal bureaucracies cognizant of, or responsible for, U.S. civil/industrial security affairs (education, transportation, environmental protection, health and human services, agriculture, safety, etc.). The full public accountability of Washington's management of its increased investments for civil/industrial improvements would very likely spark more positive, grass-roots participation by more Americans. Challenges and opportunities for fulfillment of individuals' enlightened self-interests in improving U.S. civil/industrial security affairs would become more apparent. Consequently, Americans would probably demonstrate a moral reawakening in their concerns for national security. Washington leaders could reduce their costly, secretive, punitive, divisive and ineffective security efforts to fight wars against the enemies of crime, drugs, poverty and ignorance in the United States—all because of the strengthened integrity of infrastructure-support systems.

Thus there would be a three-stage process for reforming U.S. security. First, U.S. policy and programs for military/industrial cooperation with allies would spread, balance and reduce the burden of defense of Western democracies in meeting military security requirements for their interdependence and growth in relations with Soviet bloc and nonaligned nations. Second, Washington's open democratic cooperation with state, regional and community governments would increase U.S. educational, human and environmental health and safety, housing resources and transportation capabilities for managing stability and growth in civil/industrial interdependence, employment, income and markets so that burdens of moral disintegration (crime, drugs, poverty and ignorance) would be reduced and domestic security requirements of the U.S. Constitution would be fulfilled more effectively. The third stage would be a Marshall Plan revival for Western democracies to build bonds of political, economic and industrial interdependence with nonaligned Third World nations—details of which are expounded in the next chapter. The remainder of this chapter concerns highlights of U.S. infrastructure improvements and their contributions to U.S. manufacturers' revival.

U.S. University, Government and Civil/Industrial Complex

The Morrill Act of Congress in 1863 gave birth to interdependent efforts by U.S. land-grant universities of agricultural and mechanical arts, government agricultural agencies (federal, state and county), farmers and U.S. manufacturers. As a result of those efforts, U.S. production and domestic and export marketing of agricultural products have been managed very effectively. Americans have acquired and sustained world-class competitiveness from the U.S. agricultural, industrial and university complex for 125 years! There is little doubt that U.S. manufacturers who are members of this complex have achieved and sustained top rankings in global competitiveness, product innovations and process productivity. Thus there are significant and useful precedents for establishing and operating a U.S. university, government and civil/industrial complex to revive U.S. manufacturers' global competitiveness in markets for consumer/industrial products.

Perhaps at the outset of discussing this proposal, issues or problems of complicity by the university with affairs of industry and government and, relatedly, issues of class distinctions between publicly funded universities and more prestigious, private universities should be acknowledged. These latter issues have for a long time been anachronistic myths, or meaningless pejoratives for contrasting the quality of the work of "cow colleges" with that of "ivy league" institutions. The development and application of knowledge is the common, identical purpose of all colleges and universities, whether funded by taxpayers, foundations, wealthy alumni, industry or government.

However, as an educational institution, the university, whether public or private, is chartered by society and, therefore, must strive to research, develop and disseminate knowledge freely for the sake of all peoples' enlightenment. Industrial firms strive for knowledge to gain proprietary information and competitive (or exclusive) rights or advantages of new knowledge applied to their innovations of products or processes. Governments have political or military interests in the power of knowledge and control of its uses. The age of expanded efforts, increased investments and more rapid development and application of the science and technology of material, energy and information have put the university, inextricably, in the role as the wellspring for knowledge industries, whose bonds of interdependence with manufacturers and governments must grow stronger, because of mutual security requirements for innovations and competitiveness based substantially (but not exclusively) on science or technology.

A compromise of this conflict of interest would be for the university to refuse grants or contracts and development of information for *military purposes* but to accept grants or contracts for *civil/industrial purposes* of manufacturers or government and to insist, as a condition of its contract agreement, on retaining patent ownership and control of fees and full dissemination developed via efforts of all grants or contract agreements with industrial firms and government agencies. Accordingly, the university might offer licenses and full dissemination of its patented information for use by all manufacturers and governments (U.S. or foreign). Except under the most unusual circumstances stipulated in the contract agreement and for very limited time periods, it might license early exclusive use of such information by sponsors of research grants or contracts. Such arrangements offer the mutual advantages of interdependence among manufacturers, universities and governments.

In effect, manufacturers would join in funding the support of research facilities and educational efforts by universities, perhaps with tax exemptions for their philanthropic support. Manufacturers would avoid costly duplications of their own research organizations that might otherwise be required. They also gain the advantage of experience with and knowledge of graduate students and faculty, who might significantly contribute to their plans for new technology and innovations. Not least, they would probably be exempted from antitrust laws, because of their cooperation and support of university research, even though, as direct competitors, manufacturers would stand to gain from the same research efforts by the university.

Universities would gain from their advancement of science and technology, which would more likely be relevant to real-world needs of industrial and economic improvements, and from their knowledge of uses (and abuses) of technology by manufacturers or governments. They would also gain income from patents, license fees, grants and contracts funded by governments and manufacturers and from expanded relations with alumni, government officials and industry.

Federal, state and local governments, along with associations of different manufacturers, could coordinate their amounts and uses of funds so that they would be invested equitably among all U.S. universities and would also provide adequately for all or most of the specialized, research and development needs of manufacturers of products designed with mature and new technologies of materials, energy and information systems. The point here is to emphasize decentralized, pluralistic and participatory management of a U.S. university, government and civil/industrial complex in all 50 states, according to the needs for research and development of different kinds of technology used by manufacturers. Dual political and economic security requirements, institutional interdependence and different kinds of technological improvements can be managed effectively and have been demonstrated by the experiences of the U.S. agricultural, industrial, government and university complex. In addition to contributions to food-products manufacturers, that complex is developing improvements for human and environmental health.

Ostensive purposes of Washington's investments in the proposed, civil/industrial university complex would be to fulfill national security requirements for U.S. manufacturers' revival. However, achievement of those purposes would most likely be ensured by channeling those investments so they are managed primarily by American universities, not by the bureaucracies of U.S. industry or the U.S. government. American universities are wellsprings of knowledge capabilities, which are vital necessities not only for developing and managing new and appropriate technology for American manufacturers to exploit, but also for young Americans, while pursuing their chosen courses of higher education, *to practice* the disciplines of enlightened self-governance and preservation of democratic freedom. Thus while investing more U.S. taxpayers' dollars to revive U.S. manufacturers' competitiveness, those funds would also be used to revive the quality of U.S. education. By working with manufacturers for civil/industrial improvements, universities would become more active and more politically and economically accountable for managing the development and application of *appropriate technologies*. Appropriate technologies are those that conserve nature's environmental qualities and serve both to liberate and to unite (and not divide, repress or destroy) global humanity.

The university's expanded involvement with civil/industrial improvements would require interdisciplinary efforts by faculty with students of several, if not many, different academic departments in order for its research and development processes to result in appropriate technologies for manufacturers to exploit. Those improvements should be appropriate qualities for product developers, product designers, process designers and customers of manufacturers as well as for preserving human and environmental health. While communicating periodically with those technical specialists of the real world, the university's counterpart specialists would work together and simultaneously (instead of separately and sequentially) to sustain their focus

142   Manufacturing for Security of the U.S.

holistically on the purposes of quality improvements. Thus the
university would use more democratic and experiential methods
of conducting research and development projects for U.S. manufacturers' improvements in a manner complementary with the
methods of participatory management by workers, technical specialists and executives of manufacturing firms. Of course, preventive and remedial measures of technical, economic, social
and legal accountability would be essential for managing the
university's efforts and progress toward the goals of appropriate
technology. Consequently, those measurements would very
likely involve faculty and students of the university's departments of sociology, law, economics, management and political
science for those measures and consensus about their mutual
relationships to be intellectually sound and acceptable for industry and government.

Thus the role and missions of U.S. manufacturers to provide
better products for more people to live and work together more
productively would become more interdependent and fused
with the role and mission of U.S. universities: to develop and
disseminate knowledge serving societies' immediate and long-
term needs for enlightened self-governance and universal truths.
Both institutions would become more effective from their more
extensive and intensive concrete relationships. And because universities and manufacturers uniquely are pivotal institutions determining key conditions for the security and progress by other
institutions of our industrialized society, it follows that domestic
and foreign security affairs would be enhanced for all Americans.

To improve the moral and intellectual qualities of university
education is to improve those qualities for all levels of education.
There have to be logical, progressive relationships among the
scope, depth and pedagogy of curricula at universities, high
schools, middle schools, elementary schools and even kinder-
garten and nursery schools. University curricula and experiences
by professors and teachers exert exemplary influences over curricula and experiences of students in the lower levels of education. University involvement with manufacturers' civil/
industrial improvements would be influential, even inspirational
for young students in elementary schools. The democratic, participatory management and accounting for human resources as
assets (instead of as expenditures to be avoided) would provide

moral and intellectual enlightenment about life and work by all other institutions dependent on universities and manufacturing firms. Thus evolving from the U.S. civil/industrial and university complex there could be reductions in social problems of resignation, cynicism, school dropouts, poverty, unemployment and drug addiction among the American youth.

These potential, yet achievable advantages per se would seem to be the justification for Washington leaders to invest more in university research, education and management of a civil/industrial complex for U.S. manufacturers' revival using the precedent of the 125 years of the successful experience of universities developing knowledge for managing the U.S. agricultural industrial complex.

Ironically, Washington politicians and Americans, generally, tend to ignore the significance of their universities' contributions to productivity and world-class competitiveness of the U.S. agricultural industrial complex. As noted earlier, faculty and students of older, more traditional (e.g., ivy league) universities rejected concerns of land-grant colleges of agricultural and mechanical arts, because their curricula were considered too mundane, too practical and too devoid of the intellectual qualities of classical arts and scientific knowledge. Even after those colleges grew and transformed into eminent public universities, the significance of contributions by their agricultural colleges continued to be ignored. Yet those contributions continued dramatically to increase the productivity, product innovations, markets and income of the U.S. agricultural industrial complex. Perhaps those contributions have been ignored not only because of the patronizing snobbery by larger numbers of faculty and students in arts, sciences and professional schools of privately endowed American universities, but also because contributions by agricultural colleges have affected such a dramatic decrease in population and employment by American farms as to reduce their significance in political or economic terms. However, the U.S. agricultural, industrial and university complex has a history of worthy precedents applicable for governments (federal, state, regional, local), universities and industries to work together for civil/industrial innovations and competitiveness by U.S. manufacturers.

The significance of the American university's complicity with

Washington's military/industrial complex tends also to be ignored, albeit for different reasons. Universities have suffered moral disintegration, intellectual divisiveness and even physical violence (resulting in deaths at Kent State University), because of the violations of academic freedom and responsibility for full, open accountability and free dissemination of knowledge from research and development projects by university faculty and students. The Pentagon's military requirements for secrecy and its military purposes of science and technological power for deterrence and destruction remain intolerable with requirements and purposes of university research and education. Yet, the conflict between purposes and accountability of Pentagon research and those of university research continues unresolved, or tends to be ignored, because universities have been forced to rely more and more on federal funds managed by the Pentagon. About 65 percent of federal funds for research and development during the 1980s were planned and controlled by Pentagon bureaucrats.[2] And Pentagon funds far exceeded those made available to universities by foundations, industries or state governments for faculty and students to research and develop technology for civil/industrial improvements and to keep faith with traditional university requirements for the academic freedom of information. The decline in quality of American higher education has been acknowledged. Allan Bloom complained about the closing of the American mind, former Secretary of Education William Bennett accused universities of the failure to control the costs of their research and teaching programs and the American Academy of Sciences warned of the dangers of the decline in the number of American graduates in the fields of science and engineering. All of these concerns are strongly linked with the conflicts of purpose and accountability for university research funded by the Pentagon in violation of academic freedom, which is a basic requirement for the security and progress of universities.

The Pentagon also expanded its role in managing the research and development of civilian technology of U.S. manufacturers, by launching its programs for HDTV, high-temperature superconductors and microelectronic computer chips. But those programs are not likely to be effective, again because technology improvements require open democratic processes of participatory management. These requirements are practically impossible for the Pentagon to tolerate, because of its highest priority requirement for military deterrence and secrecy. The Pentagon's program to develop the Sergeant York radar-guided antiaircraft gun expended $1.8 billion, but the gun failed to perform and the program had to be cancelled. In 1980, the Pentagon launched a $1 billion program to build super-fast computer chips needed for military communications and weapons systems. By 1987 the "superchips" had been put into only one military system. Meanwhile, Japanese manufacturers had developed superchips for civilian electronic products already available in global markets. The U.S. Air Force B–1 bombers, costing $230 million each, and the U.S. Navy Aegis cruisers and destroyers, costing more than $80 billion, were produced, but with radar systems that kept them operationally defective for years after they were delivered to the Air Force and Navy commands. Experts have noted that civilian technology improvements are increasingly surpassing military technology improvements. Propulsion and navigational controls of civilian ships are more highly automated and require fewer people than those of U.S. Navy ships.[3]

Thus from their work with the Pentagon's research and development programs, U.S. manufacturers and universities have suffered not just from the high costs, long delays and ineffective results of their research and development projects, they have also suffered serious erosions of their institutional vitality sustained only by processes for open democratic, competitive management and accountability—processes that are inimical to those required by the Pentagon. Since World War II, Washington leaders have deceived themselves, harmed American manufacturers and universities and made America less secure because they believed in the myths of spin-off advantages and committed top-priority funds for universities and manufacturers to conduct research and development of technological improvements for military deterrence. It is for these reasons that federal and state governments and U.S. manufacturers should invest more funds for civil/industrial research and development contracts with universities.

A nationwide, civil/industrial and university complex would provide more than the basic research or advanced technology for U.S. manufacturers to improve their products, processes and competitiveness. Its management would obviate the need for a national industrial policy conducted by a federal bureaucracy and restore the moral integrity and vitality of institutional contributions to American freedom and security, locally and globally.

Appropriate Technology for Manufacturers

During recent decades, U.S. manufacturers have utilized technologies for their products or processes, unintentionally, to cause serious harm to human health and safety. A few well-known examples are General Motors' Chevrolet Corvair, Ford Motor Company's Ford Pinto, Johns-Manville's asbestos products and Hooker Chemical Company's disposal of process wastes. These experiences provoked organized reactions by public interest groups, including Ralph Nader's consumer-protection organizations and the Sierra Club. And political pressures by those groups led to the establishment of regulatory bureaucracies in Washington, notably the Environmental Protection Agency and the Consumer Product Safety Commission that have authority to mandate requirements for manufacturers to change the technology of their products or processes to protect human or environmental health and safety. Thus free-enterprise competitive and market economic forces have not been adequate, because political and legal forces and Washington bureaucrats have also become involved in defining appropriate technology for manufacturers' products or processes.

Increased government interventions and regulations have raised adversarial qualities in relations among manufacturers, customers and factory communities, because legal (i.e., governmental) processes for defining appropriate technology require adversarial relationships between the prosecutor and defender of the technology that manufacturers must innovate under the rules of free competitive market accountability. Consequently, scholars, business journalists and U.S. manufacturers have argued that added costs of technology regulations have been a major cause of the decline in U.S. manufacturers' competitive standing. (Of course, defenders of such regulations argue that foreign manufacturers have had both to comply with those regulations and to compete effectively with U.S. manufacturers.) Manufacturers and consumer and environmental-protection organizations have lobbied for Washington leaders to relax or to strengthen the government's regulations of appropriate technology for products and processes. While costs, controversies, political and economic complexities have increased, the strength of Americans' consensus or commitments to changing definitions of appropriate technology probably declined, to the detriment of U.S. manufacturers.

Of course, American youth are most vitally affected by the issues of appropriate technology because their resolutions or definitions affect the Constitutional freedom for posterity. The proposal to expand the role of the American universities in research and development of appropriate technology would mean that university students would more actively assume greater responsibilities and would be made more rigorously accountable for their own future health and safety. Thus students would exert a concrete role in self-governing conditions affecting their own destinies. Developing and advancing research and technology are already acknowledged as accomplishments increasingly by young faculty and students. By working together with their faculty and in consultation with U.S. manufacturers, students could invigorate intellectual and cooperative processes for deciding and defining appropriate technology for manufacturers, and thus affect a very desirable diversion from legalist and adversarial processes and from the roles of lobbyists, politicians and bureaucrats in Washington. Such diversion would lead to significant advantages for all Americans. There would be more civility and intellectual (and less partisan and divisive) engagement and resolution of controversies over questions of technological, social or economic advantages and effects on human or environmental health and safety or over costs of prevention versus costs of remedies from hazards caused by changes in manufacturers' technology. Relations between government and manufacturers would be improved for the benefit and trust of society as a whole, because pressures for lobbying, threats or bribery would be reduced, if not eliminated. Existing intellectual talents, resources and peer-review processes by university faculty and students would be used practically and seriously, not just for academic recognition, but for enlightening self-governance of local and global concerns that technology always serves human needs and conserves environmental resources, before they are defined as appropriate. Americans' consensus and commitments to appropriate technology so defined would be significantly strengthened, and consequently, their support for American manufacturers would very likely increase.

This is not to suggest that universities should replace federal regulatory agencies responsible for manufacturers' compliance with standards for protecting people and the environment, but rather that universities would become more actively involved in the process of defining those standards, as a consequence of their expanded work for civil/industrial technological innovation. Industry, government and the American people would want more participation by universities to enlighten and resolve issues about the effects of technological innovation. The purpose of each and every civil/industrial research project would require that university scientists and engineers work to innovate technology that is healthy and safe, not just more powerful, efficient or economical for manufacturers and their customers. Such a purpose would also require that *all* faculty, students and university administrators hold their colleagues explicitly accountable for achieving that purpose in the processes for self-governance, recognition and reward for contributions to their university's moral and intellectual integrity and development of relations with industries and government.

For federal and state governments and U.S. manufacturers, the costs of expanding the role of U.S. universities in defining appropriate technology would be offset by savings from reducing lobbying or litigation expenses and the costs of the efforts by government technicians. Universities already possess the full range of intellectual, faculty and student capabilities required. And the faculty of agricultural colleges are already involved in efforts to improve biotechnology for improving agricultural productivity and environmental conservation. The challenges and opportunities afforded by the universities' roles in the U.S. civil/industrial complex would almost certainly affect a significant increase in the number and quality of commitments made by

American students to the variety of specialized, interdependent scientific and professional disciplines. During the 1980s, the proportion of American students enrolled in scientific and engineering disciplines declined significantly whereas the proportion of foreign students in American and foreign (especially Japanese) universities in these fields was significantly higher. This disparity raised serious concerns about the lack of future capabilities for technological innovations and managerial talents that American manufacturers would certainly need to restore their competitiveness.

In 1958, *Sputnik* prompted the U.S. government and universities to expand their commitment to improve the science and technology of the American space program. In the 1990s, the competitive growth by foreign manufacturers should prompt the federal and state governments, together with U.S. manufacturers, to expand American universities' commitment to the research and development of technology appropriate for U.S. manufacturers to improve their competitiveness.

PUBLIC INFRASTRUCTURE SYSTEMS IMPROVEMENTS

Federal savings of about $100 billion from U.S.-Soviet agreements to reduce arms expenditures and from U.S.-allied agreements to share more equitably the burdens of expenditures for conventional arms procurement and military deployment should also be reinvested in public infrastructure improvements: highways, railways, air transportation, space systems, health, housing, education, welfare, water resources and solid waste facilities.

The quality capabilities of the U.S. infrastructure systems have declined since 1965. They were neglected because of the demands of the Vietnam War and its aftermath of chronic inflation during the 1970s, the trillions of dollars expended for the unprecedented peacetime military buildup and, in the 1980s, the Reagan administration's reductions of expenditures for Richard Nixon's new federalism programs and Lyndon Johnson's great society programs. State and local governments struggled to finance and maintain, but were unable to improve, public infrastructures because they suffered the loss of revenues from the decline of U.S. manufacturers' competitiveness; the decline of real per capita earnings of Americans; and the rise of costs associated with poverty, crime, drugs and public safety and, not least, because the federal government's predominant powers of taxation, financing and control of operational interdependencies of U.S. public infrastructure systems.

Federal investments to improve those systems are vital requirements for supporting U.S. manufacturers' efforts to improve their competitive capabilities. Perhaps most important is that infrastructure improvements are the political opportunities Washington leaders need and the market opportunities U.S. weapons manufacturers need to convert from military/industrial to civilian/industrial operations, with minimum losses of employment and income for Americans no longer needed by the shrinking military/industrial establishment. Infrastructure improvements are new, national security requirements of the 1990s and the twenty-first century.

It would be foolish to suggest a total amount of federal funds or amounts of their allocated expenditures for different kinds of infrastructure improvements throughout the 50 states. Such a suggestion would be tantamount to national economic planning and blatant denials of democratic freedom and the obligation of manufacturers and government. Moreover, a U.S. weapons manufacturer unable to decide and manage product changes to suit the needs for public infrastructure improvements is not ever likely to become a manufacturer of consumer/industrial equipment serving the needs of competitive U.S. and foreign markets. Unfortunately, the Pentagon years of political, military and pork barrel funding and procurements may have caused an incurable indolence for some U.S. defense contractors.

However, it might be useful to point out that the need for U.S. infrastructure improvements offers a full range of production and marketing opportunity for high-technology and low-technology manufacturers of military equipment. For example, manufacturers of Army ground combat vehicles might consider the construction of high-speed rail-passenger transportation equipment needed for the urban and metropolitan areas of the Northeast and Far West or producing equipment for repairs or construction of schools, low-cost housing, waste control or waste disposal facilities. Contractors developing high-technology equipment for strategic defense initiatives (SDI) or electronic systems for navigation, communications or weapons fire controls might consider manufacturing equipment for space communications, weather information, commercial air-traffic control systems or medical diagnostic equipment. And contract manufacturers of nuclear materials for weapons and military reactors might be best qualified by their experiences to develop materials, equipment or facilities for the disposal and control of nuclear wastes and for more safe and efficient production and utilization of nuclear energy.

By working with all levels of government to improve networks of public infrastructure facilities and organizations, manufacturers would reduce political and economic difficulties and expedite solutions to political and economic problems for the U.S. government to change its security strategy and for manufacturers to convert the purpose of their products and processes from those of military deterrence. Defense contractors could more easily exploit advantages of employees' participation in the management of their conversion from military markets. Employees' participation would be free from restrictions of military secrecy, security clearances and classified information about technology for design, production and operation of products. And with much more enthusiasm, their engineers, technical staff and rank-and-file employees would probably dedicate their efforts to new products serving the productive needs of civilians in their own communities and to the rewards (tangible and intangible) from the open accountability and acknowledgment of their efforts. In these times of declining risks and rising opportunities for post–cold war relationships and for fulfilling socioeconomic security requirements, probably most, if not all, stakeholders of U.S. military products manufacturers would actively support their conversions to civilian markets.

Manufacturers, cooperating with government, would be able to minimize the loss of industrial jobs and income for their employees. They would also be able to provide civilian jobs for Americans discharged or retiring from military duties. Manufacturers' financial and marketing opportunities would be expanded, because all levels of government as well as foundations and private welfare institutions would participate in the infrastructure improvement programs. Economic growth potentials of civilian markets are many times greater than those of military markets, because of the larger number and variety of interdependent demands of participants (employees, financiers, customers and taxpayers) in civilian markets.

The nationwide funding of infrastructure improvements by government and eleemosynary institutions and the modern technology of the equipment offered by manufacturers to provide for those improvements would very likely affect significant changes in the national networks of organizations and facilities. For example, community governments might form consortia to acquire and operate a single, regional facility and organization for managing water resources and sewage disposals, public transportation or solid-waste recycling and disposal facilities. Similarly, city government might combine with suburban governments to acquire and utilize economically common facilities for public (mass) transportation, health, welfare, employment, family counseling, child-care services or maintenance of public roads, buildings and housing facilities. The point is that to take advantage of technological and productivity improvements offered by manufacturers' equipment (and their methods of operation and maintenance support), all levels government would probably reform and combine their infrastructure organization and facilities to provide various public services required by their constituents. Thus, in effect, manufacturers' marketing efforts and products would improve the *scope and integrity* of U.S. networks of public service organizations and facilities. This would be accomplished in a manner analogous to the way in which U.S. and foreign manufacturers have been the major impetus for their respective governments to strengthen their bonds of political and economic interdepedence and to form common markets with common currencies and with (democratically prescribed) common rules to account for performance by business, industrial and government organizations responsive to the expectations of those markets in Western Europe and North America and probably in the Asian Rim countries as well.

The effects of improving the integrity and effectiveness of U.S.

public services would far transcend the political economies of their cost reductions per se. Even more important, those effects would also be very likely to reduce costs of Americans' social disintegration that have been growing steadily and alarmingly during recent decades: alienation, drugs, school dropouts, teenage pregnancies, crime, etc. Americans' social integrity would probably be improved along with improved infrastructure organizations and facilities and the common sharing of their services by the people from affluent suburbs, gentrified residential areas and ethnic residential areas or the poor of inner cities. I can only offer the suggestion, not empirical evidence, that if all or most Americans work together to improve and share the common services of education, transportation, public works public welfare, and health the costs of wars against povert teenage pregnancies, crime and drugs would very likely be duced. In producing common, integrated infrastructure provements, U.S. manufacturers would very likely unit Americans—rich and poor; black, white, Hispanic and As in managing the industrial revolution of rising expectatior rising capabilities.

NOTES

1. R. E. McGarrah, *Study of the NATO Hawk Program* (W D.C.: Logistics Management Institute, 1965), 391–432.

2. William J. Broad, "Military Research Facing the P' Budgets," *The New York Times*, July 3, 1989, pp. 1, B7.

3. Ibid.

6

U.S. Marshall Plan Revival: Programs to Boost Manufacturers' Exports and Close Gaps with Third World Nations

History teaches that power and conflict are inherent elements of relations among people, institutions and nations. And the lessons of recent history are that the growth in power from manufacturers' products has escalated the requirements for more peaceful conflicts and uses of those products. Vietnam and Afghanistan, *perestroika* and *glasnost* and U.S.-Soviet arms reductions have indicated the decline in geopolitical power from weapons and military force. The rising influence of West Germany and Japan has indicated the need for industry and government to shift their security strategies and increase their political and economic power to more peaceful contentions in the markets for consumer and industrial products. The game of international security affairs has been changing, so the U.S. government should increase its support of manufacturers' exports of consumer/industrial products and reduce its support of their exports of military equipment.

To fulfill new national security requirements for U.S. manufacturers' revival, it is not sufficient for the government to reinvest all the prospective savings from U.S.-Soviet arms reductions and from U.S.-allied military/industrial cooperation in a new

U.S. civil/industrial and university complex for research and development of new technology and in infrastructure improvements. Washington should invest a substantial proportion of those savings in a Marshall Plan revival to boost its manufacturers' export opportunities and to close the gaps with Third World nations.

As pointed out earlier, U.S. trade deficits are not likely to be reduced and U.S. manufacturers' competitiveness is not likely to be revived by Washington's adoption of military-industrial or monetary measures to protect U.S. manufacturers' domestic and foreign trade position or by Washington's abandonment of the longstanding U.S. security strategy to promote bonds of peaceful, industrial/economic interdependence among Western democracies and industrializing nations. Moreover, the growing production volume and intensity of manufacturers' competition have nearly saturated the demands of Western markets. Therefore, to support U.S. manufacturers' revival and its security strategies for international interdependence, it is advisable for Washington to invest in Third World infrastructure programs enabling U.S. manufacturers to expand more easily and significantly their exports to markets of nonaligned countries with the greatest unfulfilled demands. Such investments are also advisable because they would help Third World societies to develop industrial/economic capabilities to repay their financial debts in full to Western nations and to be relieved of domestic, political and economic measures of increasing austerity and, consequently, from the pressures of sociopolitical violence and total collapse.

Initiatives for a Marshall Plan with Third World nations offers a more practical, positive means for Washington to support U.S. manufacturers' revival and to sustain U.S. leadership and U.S. critical mass-market responsibilities for growth in international interdependence. For Washington to invest in efforts to resist trends toward globalized, common markets with uniform rules for free, fair and open competition by industrial firms would be for all Americans not only to suffer losses of significant benefits from those markets, but also to fail to meet their Constitutional obligations for sustaining democratic liberties and responsibilities for peaceful uses of industrial powers. It is with these thoughts in mind that I invite consideration of my final proposal for reviving U.S. manufacturers' standing in global markets.

TOTAL INTEGRATED INFRASTRUCTURE SYSTEMS IMPROVEMENTS FOR THIRD WORLD NATIONS

During the decades since the fulfillment of the Marshall Plan, Congress and the White House have grown more skeptical of the effectiveness of foreign aid to developing nations. They have steadily reduced the annual percentage of U.S. GNP for foreign economic, educational or industrial assistance to levels below those of Western European allies and far below U.S. levels during the years of the Marshall Plan. They have reduced U.S. contributions to United Nations programs and ignored appeals by leaders of Third World nations for the United States to increase its investments in their efforts to build a "new international economic order."[1] Why has Washington become disillusioned with its foreign economic aid programs?

One reason is that its implementation of foreign aid policies in developing regions has been fragmented and shortsighted. Instead of providing integrated industrial, educational and economic infrastructures needed to develop self-supporting relations for rural areas and population centers, usually its foreign aid has taken the special form of *ad hoc* "gifts" (or grants) spread over vast parts of Asia, Latin America and Africa, so that they could not incite synergistic efforts or capabilities needed for self-development in Third World regions.

Another reason is that U.S. foreign aid has often been composed of gifts of cash or U.S.-produced commodities. And instead of telling the people of emerging nations that Americans were investing to develop new markets, with clear expectations of returns on their investments, those gifts represented philanthropy or patronage. Rather than encouraging and challenging the peoples of Third World nations to reciprocate by producing products or services for themselves *and* for export to strengthen the bonds of mutual interdependence, U.S. foreign aid often caused them to suffer indignities from their greater dependence on foreign aid. These indignities have led to expressions of resentment (against American colonialism or imperialism) and to U.S. reactions to reduce its aid.

U.S. foreign economic assistance also declined because of the rise of military assistance to developing nations. Decades of execution of Washington's strategies for the growth in global power for military deterrence and in U.S. arms manufacturers' requirements for industrial/economic growth resulted almost inevitably in the spread of U.S.-Soviet military confrontations and conflict by their surrogate forces in Third World nations. After all, for power to remain credible it must be exercised. U.S. and Soviet leaders demonstrated the geopolitical capability and power of the military weapons they shipped to surrogate Third World forces, to avert direct confrontations and risks of global nuclear holocaust almost certain to result from direct U.S.-Soviet military conflict. Under the economic terms of grants or trade agreements and in the name of national security requirements for deterrence or peacekeeping, they exported increasing quantities of conventional weapons to nonaligned, developing nations. However, as demonstrated by the experiences in the Middle East, Indochina, Afghanistan, Africa and Central America, forces of nonaligned nations developed and demonstrated their own power of *unconventional* uses of those weapons (i.e., repressions, insurgencies and terrorism). And, of course, these inflicted social violence and serious damage to processes in Third World nations for market development by manufacturers and foreign economic assistance by the U.S. government, other democracies and the United Nations.

Yet another important cause of the apparent ineffectiveness and decline in Washington's investments in developing nations has been the lack of coordinated efforts by the staff of different government bureaucracies, private industrial firms and nonprofit educational and health organizations to establish or develop grass-roots relations with counterpart organizations in developing countries. Pluralistic unity, mutual transactions, dedication and commitments by different socioeconomic classes and special-interest groups are habits of the American culture. They are known to be essential requirements if community and regional economic development and maintenance programs are to be effective in the United States. But they are not the cultural habits of Third World societies. So to be effective, it should be a requirement for each U.S. foreign aid program to stimulate the formation of a "critical mass" and pluralism of capabilities for a Third World society to develop its own products and processes for interdependence. And the interdependence should be both local and global so that relations within and between Third World societies and Western industrial societies are conducive to the peaceful development and use of conflict via industrial/economic competition and progress.

Democratic Organization and Management of Programs

As was suggested in chapter 4, to revive their competitive standing effectively, U.S. manufacturers have adopted more democratic participatory management by workers, technicians and executives, relaxed work rules, bureaucratic rigidities and reduced levels and influences by organizational hierarchies. Thus they have improved their market share by letting democracy work more efficiently and effectively, i.e., by encouraging all technicians, managers and workers of their firm simultaneously to focus holistically and in specific details on the corporate goals of greater flexibility, productivity and product-quality improvements (i.e., economies of change with economies of scale) for customers.

In an analogous, macroscopic manner, it is suggested that executives and grass-roots members of all levels of government, manufacturing firms, labor unions, education, health and welfare organizations could agree to participate in financing, planning, organizing and executing programs for Third World societies to close gaps more quickly and effectively and to grow more interdependent with the United States and other Western democracies. This suggestion is offered because democratic, pluralistic unity for peaceful competition and progress is the reason why the power and the standard of living of the Japanese and West German societies rapidly ascended (and those of the Soviet and Chinese societies steadily descended) in global affairs during years since World War II.

With many, if not most, Third World societies American manufacturers already have connections for import or export trade, and American business firms have connections for finance, tourism or other services. American schools and universities conduct the exchange of students, faculty and academic information, American towns and cities act as "brothers" or "sisters" in the causes for peace, health and environmental conservation, and, of course, the U.S. government has knowledge of those organized connections while it engages counterpart agencies of Third World host governments in political, military, agricultural, economic and technological and commercial affairs of mutual concern. These *connections* could be considered and utilized as basic nuclei for financing, organizing and planning United States and Third World consortia, which would execute the Marshall Plan revival program. Private and public institutional processes for serving the human needs of food, clothing, housing, education, health, transportation, energy, jobs and income would be organized and operated with their mutual relations both cooperatively and competitively, yet synergistically as they are intended to be in democratic free-market societies. Thus for the U.S.-Third World Marshall Program revival, I would propose that, instead of creating new bureaucracies, the program would build, deliberately and pragmatically on existing organized connections between the United States and a Third World society.

By using those existing, U.S.-Third World connections as basic nuclei, I do *not* mean that they should be merged together or subsumed by a single, U.S.-Marshall Plan organization under a single director for the program in each Third World nation. Instead, I mean to suggest that the U.S. government announce its intentions to launch processes for integrated public and private processes for economic development. Accordingly, Washington (perhaps, logically, the U.S. State Department) would send invitations together with offers of funds for their expenses to respond to U.S. institutions with known and desired connections with Third World nations. The invitations would invite those institutions to prepare and submit contract proposals for joint (public and private) financing, plans and operations to expand or integrate their existing connections into processes for Third World self-development and for strengthening U.S.-Third World interdependence. Each recipient institution would be apprised of other institutions to whom invitations had been sent, so that, if desired, they could consort in their proposals in response to the U.S. government. Proposal preparations would also improve joint consultations between U.S. institutions and their Third World connections. And such joint consultations could become an impetus for start-up of the development processes. Of course, the U.S. government, state governments or community governments and business and industrial firms would, together, provide all the funds and substantial proportions of the efforts, but universities and health, welfare and conservation organizations would provide staff and some funding for conducting those efforts. After agreement with the federal government, these institutions would then proceed to engage their counterparts in the Third World nations, execute their proposals for development and coordinate their efforts informally with other institutions. The U.S. State Department would require periodic reports of their progress, expenditures and problems and would release those reports to the news media. Complete open accountability and publicity of the purpose and performance of the development processes and their progress toward integrated, self-sustaining infrastructure improvements would promote interest and momentum for progress.

Also contributing to their effectiveness would be professionally trained staff of Afro-Americans, Hispanic-Americans and Asian-Americans serving in Third World (perhaps their former home) countries as representatives of American interests in the Marshall Plan revival. This would alleviate the world problem of "brain drain" and the U.S. problem of illegal immigration. For the United States to encourage ex-patriots to serve as staff members to represent either U.S. or Third World interests it would also be advantageous because they could substantially help with the inevitable problems of accommodating cultural differences between the United States and the Third World countries. In essence, this proposal is for the United States and each Third World nation to start their Marshall Plan revival by building and expanding the interdependence of their private and public connections already in existence.

The reader might logically ask how or why such a proposal

would enhance the revival of U.S. manufacturers. To respond, I would recall the initial discussion of the importance of manufacturers' products to growth in the power of interdependence. Whether the connections between the United States and a Third World society are concerned with health, education, industry, agriculture, mining or cultural exchanges, each and every one of those connections can be expanded and integrated into self-sustaining processes for *interdependence within and between the United States and the Third World society* if (and only if) together those societies would finance, produce, acquire, operate and maintain more and better products from their factories.

More transportation and communications equipment are required for more people to get together more often so they can increase the socioeconomic importance of their particular organized connection and its mission. More equipment would be needed for planting, cultivating, harvesting, processing and packaging farm crops as well as for conserving land and water resources while improving the agricultural productivity. Computers, audiovisual, chemical, biological, physical laboratory and construction equipment would be needed by those concerned with expanding the connections to improve education and health services, energy and industries for services. Of course, increased sales by those equipment manufacturers would affect increased sales by their stakeholders, i.e., manufacturers of parts, process equipment, suppliers of materials, information, capital funds and services. The number of different kinds of products or involved manufacturers is practically impossible to estimate, but the number is irrelevant. The point is that as the U.S.-Third World connections are being expanded and integrated, manufacturers' product innovations and sales would be increased and new industrial enterprises would be established, according to democratic (competitive) free-market principles, rules and processes.

The most important (nonquantifiable) characteristic of this proposed process for U.S. manufacturers' revival is the synergy of its powers of means and results: more freedom with greater interdependence among people of the United States and Third World societies; better products, better jobs and higher living standards for people and more profits for manufacturers.

There is yet another advantage of the proposed Marshall Plan revival by financing the expansion of existing U.S.-Third World–connected organizations instead of organizing a new consortium for Marshall Plan development. Unlike the Marshall Plan of Europe during the 1950s, many, if not most, foreign aid efforts by the U.S. government have involved the establishment of new project organizations. A U.S. Agency for International Development (U.S.A.I.D.) project organization and its counterpart Third World organization are established to manage the project. In effect these organizations act as channels for U.S. funds to people of Third World societies. Too often, problems arise because of the direction and quantity of funds flowing through such channels. The direction is from the top, down, i.e., from the hierarchy of central government to peasants, health workers, tradesmen, etc. Consequently, the funds become "trickle-down," because, in keeping with traditions for bureaucratic growth, government organizations expend those funds *first* for increasing their own staff, *then* for services intended for their clientele. Project overhead and administrative expenses for employing government bureaucrats are higher and expenditures to defray Third World economic improvements are lower than desired or necessary. Moreover, the services of the project are likely to overlap and be competitive (not complementary) with services already being rendered by other U.S. organizations working to aid the Third World society. Those latter organizations are the pluralistic, more efficient, middle-class nucleus for a Marshall Plan revival by the United States because they are concerned with both financial and operational processes for Third World improvements; and their staffs would work more closely with their respective Third World-counterpart staff connections. And compared to ad hoc Federal bureaucracies, their financial and operational performances accountability can be just as rigorous and precise (and even more open and objective), because their transactions and operations would be conducted in the open, for the press and interested citizens to examine. Washington's needs for the information feedback would not be staffed by bureaucrats, but instead, facilitated by electronic telecommunications equipment. American taxpayers' funds would be invested in contracts with existing organized U.S. connections for reviving manufacturers' exports and for Marshall Plan development of Third World countries. And purposes could be achieved more quickly and effectively, with lower costs.

U.S.-Allied Cooperation for Third World Improvements

The U.S. could also initiate proposals for Western industrial democracies to convert or adapt their experiences with military/industrial cooperation (as described in chapter 5) to multilateral programs for closing their gaps of living standards expanding their industrial and financial transactions with Third World countries. There are significant advantages to this strategy for a Marshall Plan revival.

Political and diplomatic groundwork has already been set for this strategy. At their summit meeting in Paris, July, 1989, the leaders of the group of seven western democracies (Canada, France, Italy, Japan, the UK, the United States and West Germany) acknowledged their challenge and obligations with Third World nations. The group of seven nations could afford and manage the largest investments for more rapid Third World improvements. Western nations would sustain their political and economic bonds of mutual interdependence and their common defense markets created by their programs for military/industrial cooperation. From those programs they would have gained experience and precedent for industrial and economic development and would manage international trade and currency payments, while sustaining technology improvements and competition by manufacturers' firms of partner nations. These precedents could serve to accelerate the closing of the gaps between industrial democracies and developing nations. Compared with bilateral efforts to close the gaps with Third World nations, U.S.-allied, multilateral efforts would relieve manufacturers from critics' accusations that Western Europeans were trying to revive their power of colonialist domination of the recently freed nations of Africa and Asia or that the United States was trying to restore its "banana republic" relationships with the nations of Central America. Also from the point of view of U.S. manufacturers, this multilateral strategy for a Marshall Plan revival would offer more programs and larger export market opportunities to fill the huge demands of Third World societies. And, of course, as it would in bilateral programs, the U.S. government would provide financial incentives of Overseas Private Investment Corporation (OPIC) guarantees of federal insurance against the risks of losses from their investments in overseas operations in Third World nations, pursuant to their participation in multilateral programs.

Thus U.S.-allied cooperation for Third World improvements would strengthen the post–cold war momentum for peace and security via industrial interdependence and growth of common markets, North and South as well as East and West. The importance of this strategic advantage needs to be emphasized.

Growing prospects for East-West military reductions in Europe prompted President George Bush to suggest that the U.S. government might withdraw not only its military forces but also its political influences so that Western European governments would be left alone to form their own political and economic policies for encouraging Eastern European countries' efforts to leave the Soviet bloc.[2] If these suggestions were to be carried out, it would be most unfortunate for U.S. and Western European manufacturers. Because they have the greatest stake in preserving and increasing the momentum for growth of the common worldwide markets, their security and progress are derived from the geographical and international interdependence produced by their products. U.S. manufacturers need the U.S. government's political, legal and economic support of each and every one of their industrial and financial efforts in the world market.

Economic problems and declining requirements for geopolitical security via military forces should not prompt the U.S. government to abandon requirements for geopolitical security via U.S. manufacturers' operations. U.S. industrial firms have grown to become the major inextricable contributors to the European Common Market of 1992, and Western European industries have become inextricable contributors to the North Atlantic Common Market already in existence. If the U.S. government is to serve the industrial and economic security interests of all Americans, then it must continue to exert its influence and support for the U.S. manufacturers' share of growth in the common markets.

The reduction in requirements for NATO military forces should not mean a reduction in requirements for U.S.-Western European political and economic interdependence so vital to manufacturers' security and progress. While East-West military reductions are gradually executed, U.S.-allied military/industrial cooperation would further reduce U.S. economic problems and strengthen Western solidarity. With participation in Europe by the U.S. government together with U.S. manufacturers, challenges and opportunities of political and economic reunification and industrial trade by Eastern and Western Europe would be managed with fewer risks from failures of *perestroika*, and consequent risks of future Soviet military interventions in Eastern Europe. U.S.-NATO military/industrial cooperation would eliminate the nationalistic pressure for the uncontrolled distribution of weapons and growth in financial loans, defaults in repayments and threats of political and economic collapse by societies of nonaligned nations. The U.S. government must support its manufacturers' growth and revival of their peaceful uses of competitiveness in all markets of the world.

CHALLENGES AND OPPORTUNITIES OF A MARSHALL PLAN REVIVAL

Challenges and opportunities are matters of the decision makers' perception, reflection and understanding. So comments on attitudes about a Marshall Plan revival could enhance possibilities for its effective adoption.

People make markets for people (not for money or products). So the largest markets in the world are yet to be made in Asia, Africa and Latin America, where most of the world's people live. And people make markets by using and exchanging ideas and things, which *a priori* they hold to be valuable, not by acts of patronage or charity but, of course, by market transaction.

Many Americans reflect on the Marshall Plan as a program that helped Europeans recover from the damages of World War II. But this is not a valid reflection. Most essentially, and from its inception, the Marshall Plan was a two-way marketing trans-action. For in his speech at Harvard University, General George Marshall proposed a market transaction by requesting Europe-ans to indicate the things (capital funds, equipment, food, sup-plies and services) they would need *and* requesting Americans to indicate the things they would provide. Americans' response was certainly not philanthropy nor was it an investment to re-store the pre–World War II conditions of European markets. Instead, Americans and Europeans bargained and committed to self-interested terms for market transactions to develop their huge foreign market holdings, and their interdependent market relations for progress sharing and peacekeeping by the North Atlantic community of nations.

It is a tradition, perhaps still a strong cultural habit of Asians, Africans and Latin Americans to bargain together *before* exchang-ing valuables. In other words, as a prerequisite for each market transaction, they engage first in communicating their diverging, then converging, attitudes about the value of their respective belongings, both tangible and intangible. In effect, their bar-gaining is a necessary process for gaining mutual respect, trust or human agreement before binding mutual commitments to the exchange are enacted.

By contrast, Americans have automated and displaced habits of bargaining. Multimedia advertising, supermarket merchan-dising and automatic checkout counters have almost completely eliminated necessities for human bargaining. And of course, markets of industrialized societies are so full of merchandise necessities that there is no time for people to spend bargaining before each and every transaction they commit. Increasingly, scientized methods (statistical sampling for market research and market experimental testing) have been substituted for human, buyer-seller bargaining, as prerequisites for American market transaction. However, Americans have paid for those substi-tutions. As rather clearly indicated by the rise in consumer move-ments, the number and cost of litigation cases of product performance reliability and manufacturers' liability, those pro-cesses (with their inherent, socioscientific power) may also be sociooperant conditioners legally invalid for buyers' acceptance of sellers' terms and condition, because they are not genuinely bargained, bilateral terms for market transactions. Consequently, scientific methods for market development may become deceptions of trust and mutual respect that are inherent in bargaining requirements for genuine, free-market transactions and stronger bonds of interdependence. Moreover, these comments also relate to the ironies of processes for free democratic political elections. The rising power of scientifically trained, sociopolitical conditioners and the power of special-interest citizens' adversarial groups have had the ironic effects of rising apathy and declining numbers of citizens who vote in American elections.

The point of these matters is that by engaging in *genuine bargaining* with counterpart representatives of Third World societies over conditions for an effective Marshall Plan revival, Americans would not only enhance their success, they would also revive their own traditional humanitarian values of trust, morality and toleration. At the same time they would reduce their costs of suspicion, intolerance, litigation and divisiveness.

Processes of industrialization have imbued Americans with the idea that "bigger is better." Accordingly, they developed their mass technologies and large investments for production and distribution of energy and agricultural products and, until a few years ago, for bigger and better main frame computers and automobiles. But if Americans engage in genuine Marshall Plan bargaining with developing societies, they might learn and benefit from more appropriate technology. Certainly, the Marshall Plan and appropriate technology will be more effective for U.S. Third World partners to develop their own capabilities for economic interdependence.

For example, Maheshwar Dayal, who built India's first atomic reactor, brought solar-powered electricity to at least 5,000 poor villages as well as solar water heaters to the hotels and hospitals of New Delhi. Dayal also managed the production of solar-powered batteries for city buses and energy plantations of fast-growing trees, sowed to mitigate the loss of 3.7 million acres of forest. And 1.2 million rural Indian families have been switched to biogas cooking, using wood and animal wastes.[3] Surely solar energy technology deserves more serious consideration and application in the United States in light of the growing concerns about energy shortages and the human and environmental safety hazards of its massive, centralized power systems.

American mass technology has increased human productivity and expanded product varieties from agricultural processes. Costs of American foods have been low, while their availability has remained higher than that required for U.S. needs and provided for its export market opportunities and trade credits. But among the social consequences have been chronic unemployment, family disintegration, educational dropouts, illiteracy, poverty and racial violence in urban areas, and among the environmental consequences have been topsoil erosion, deforestation and agrichemical and pesticide poisoning of animals, plants and humans in rural areas. Is American mass technology appropriate for developing social, agricultural and economic capabilities and for preserving environmental conditions in Third World nations? Dayal said, "Development needs a change in focus, with not so much of it coming from the top," and he described a village in Rajasthan where he introduced solar-powered lighting.

They never had any lights in their history. They told me "You have literally brought light into our world." Their days are longer. They can have a farmers' literacy program at the end of the day. Doctors can treat the sick at night. . . . Solar systems can also be used for cooking, crop-drying, stills and kilns.[4]

Dayal might have added other significant advantages of his appropriate energy technology and equipment for rural villages in India. The facts that solar-powered lighting enables peasants to engage in literacy programs and treat their sick at night would engender conditions and desires by the poor to control population growth and to increase their productivity and participation in markets.

A Marshall Plan revival should be bargained, formulated and executed as a democratic, free enterprise process for the enlightened self-interest of Americans and people of Third World societies in their growth of industrial power, progress and freedom. A Marshall Plan revival is also a process for Western industries and governments to prevent the spread, or to reduce entrenchment, of Soviet Marxist-Leninist power in nonaligned nations much more effectively than the Western process of military/industrial deterrence.

This raises another kind of challenge, or opportunity, namely, the choice of Third World nations with which to engage in a Marshall Plan revival. The prospective advantages and strengths of existing, organized connections are not the same for U.S. or Western governments and manufacturers in all Third World nations. The choice of nations with which to launch strategies for the Marshall Plan revival is important because effective efforts in those initial programs could prejudice chances that later programs would be effective. Unlike military/industrial programs for Soviet Marxist deterrence, Marshall Plan revival programs would be conducted under the terms of an open democratic free-enterprise market accountability. And global news media reports would make the initial programs have worldwide influence.

To nominate specific, nonaligned nations with which initial programs should be launched would, of course, be presumptuous and foolish. However, some suggestions for choosing those nations might be helpful. A multilateral choice by U.S. industries and the U.S. government would be preferable to a unilateral choice by the U.S. government. Because the strategy of the Marshall Program revival is to fulfill the purpose of expansion and export growth for U.S. industry and political and economic security for the U.S. government, it would be preferable for representatives of both industries and government to participate in choosing the nonaligned Third World nations with which to launch that strategy. This suggestion is based on lessons inferred from case experiences.

In 1970, ITT-Chile attempted to persuade other U.S. companies to join in its efforts, first to prevent the election of, then the assumption of, official power and duty by President Salvadore Allende. ITT feared expropriation of its investments and nationalization of its operations by the Allende government. But Anaconda, Kennicott, Dow Chemical, Citibank and others declined, even though their Chilean investments were as large or larger and their operations were as socially and politically vital as those of ITT. However, ITT did persuade the CIA to join in its efforts. As is well known, President Salvadore Allende was assassinated by Chilean terrorists and two other Chilean officials were murdered in Washington, D.C., by terrorists.

Since 1970, Chilean citizens have suffered political and economic repressions by a military regime. Chilean-American bonds of industrial/economic interdependence have grown weaker than they probably would have been if democracy had prevailed in Chile. It is regrettable that in U.S.-Latin American affairs that have been accountable to members and markets of the United Nations, the moral, political and economic influences by ITT and the U.S. government have declined rather than increased.[5]

A lesson is that ITT and the CIA ignored or violated the principles of open democratic free-enterprise performance accountability to majority interests. Instead of representation, their actions were a violation of the majority interests expressed by U.S. business and industrial leaders, who represented American stakeholders' interests in preserving democratic processes in Chile. Thus choosing nonaligned, Third World nations with which to launch the strategies for Marshall Plan revival, this lesson could be applied effectively with participation by representatives of U.S. government (the State, Commerce, Labor, Health, Housing and Urban Development, Education, Energy and Agriculture departments) and by representatives of large and small U.S. businesses; industry, agricultural, energy, heavy or smokestack and light or high-tech manufacturers; and financial and retail or information service industries. If those representatives are willing, then they can use their power of communications technology to facilitate such participatory management of U.S. manufacturers' programs for export growth and U.S. government's programs for national security. If those numerous representatives are willing, then they could effectively use the power of communications technology to facilitate their participatory management of U.S. manufacturers' revival and conversion of U.S. power in international security affairs.

NOTES

1. The Cancun, Mexico, 1974 Conference of Third World leaders was one of several concerted political efforts by the leaders of the developing

nations of Asia, Africa and Latin America to close socioeconomic gaps with industrial democracies.

2. James M. Markham, "For Europe a New Look: Bush Fixes U.S. Role As a More Modest One," *The New York Times*, July 20, 1989, p. A9.

3. Barbara Crossette, "New Delhi Journal: Shiny Tomorrow Meets Ragged, Hungry Today," *The New York Times*, July 3, 1989, sec. A. p. 4.

4. Ibid.

5. S. Prakash Sethi, "Corporations, United States Foreign Policy and Ethics of Overseas Operations: The ITT Affair," in S. Prakash Sethi, *Up Against the Corporate Wall*, 2nd ed. (Englewood Cliffs, N.J.: Prentice-Hall, 1974).

Epilogue

Fifty years ago, U.S. manufacturers' revival occurred because they were asked to manage the growth of the world's arsenal of democracy. Their growth not only saved democracies from fascist, nationalist and socialist power, but planted and nurtured growth in the democratic power of international interdependence and industrial competitiveness.

In recent years, the Soviets have admitted the failure of Communist Marxist Socialist power, while the Japanese and West Germans have demonstrated the superiority of the power of a government and industry devoted to growth in markets for consumer/industrial products. And Third World peoples have demonstrated both their desires for joining, and their capabilities and threats for destroying, growth in common international markets for interdependence.

Clearly, U.S. politicians and U.S. manufacturers need to manage new, more appropriate technology to retain their pivotal position of leadership in international security affairs. The U.S. arsenal of democracy has become a global arms/industrial hegemony. It needs to be internationalized so that more U.S. talent and capital funds are invested in technology, processes and

products for more people to live and work together more productively under fewer threats of secrecy, distrust, divisiveness,
armed terrorism and destruction.

U.S. politicians should cease waiting for U.S. manufacturers
to develop new products and new markets, and U.S. manufacturers should cease waiting for U.S. politicians to offer new
financing for different products and customers. Instead, they
should get together with their counterparts in allied democracies
in the race to keep the world interdependent, more peaceful and
safe from the collapse of its ecological and industrial capabilities
for sustaining human and institutional progress.

Selected Bibliography

"Aircraft Industry Found to Retain Excess Capacity." *The New York Times*, January 18, 1977, pp. C41, C50.

Barzun, Jacques. *The House of Intellect*. New York: Harper and Brothers, 1959.

Broad, William J. "Military Research Facing the Pinch of Tight Budgets." *The New York Times*, July 3, 1989, pp. B1, B7.

Capdevielle, Patricia, and Neff, Arthur. "Productivity and Unit Labor Costs in the United States and Abroad." *Monthly Labor Review* (July 1975): 28–31.

Chen, G. K. C., and McGarrah, R. E. *Productivity Management: Text and Cases*. New York: CBS, Dryden, 1982.

Cleveland, Harlan. *NATO: The Transatlantic Bargain*. New York: Harper and Row, 1970.

Cohen, Stephen S., and Zysman, John. *Manufacturing Matters: Myths of the Post Industrial Society*. New York: Basic Books, 1987.

Committee for Economic Development. *Stimulating Technological Progress*. New York, 1980.

Conway, Alison Leigh. "New Dean's Proposals Raise Fears in a Yale Department." *The New York Times*, Oct. 30, 1988, p. C40.

Conway, R., and Schultz, A. "The Manufacturing Progress Function." *Journal of Industrial Engineering* (January-February 1959).

Crossette, Barbara. "The New Delhi Journal: Shiny Tomorrow Meets Ragged, Hungry Today." *The New York Times*, July 3, 1989, p. A4.

De Grasse, Robert Jr.; Murphy, Paul; and Roger, William. *The Costs and Consequences of Reagan's Military Buildup*. New York: Council on Economic Priorities, 1989.

Dreyfack, K. "Even American Motors' Knowhow is Headed Abroad." *Business Week*, March 3, 1986, p. 62.

Dricker, Peter F. *The Age of Discontinuity*. New York: Harper and Row, 1968.

Ellis, Harry B., "More Lessons From Japan." *Christian Science Monitor*, December 15, 1980, p. 1.

Fallows, James. *More Like Us: Making America Great Again*. Boston: Houghton Mifflin, 1989.

Farnsworth, Clyde H. "Panel Sees Trade Threat From Europe." *The New York Times*, June 1, 1989, p. D1.

Foust, Dean, and Roman, Monica. "Is the Boss Getting Paid Too Much?" *Business Week*, May 1, 1989, pp. 46–48.

Frank, Isaiah. *Foreign Enterprise in Developing Countries*. New York: Committee for Economic Development, 1980.

George, Susan. *Fate Worse than Debt*. New York: Grove Press, 1988.

Giamatti, A. Bartlett. *The University and the Public Interest*. New York: Athenaeum, 1981.

Guest, Robert H. "Quality of Worklife Learning." *Harvard Business Review* (July-August 1979).

Halberstam, David. *The Reckoning*. New York: Morrow, 1986.

Halloran, Richard. "Scandal Costs Lockheed $1.3 Billion in Sales to Japan." *The New York Times*, February 11, 1976, pp. 1, 76.

Hamrin, R. *Managing Growth in the 1980's*. New York: Praeger, 1980.

Hayes, Robert H., and Wheelwright, Steven C. *Restoring Our Competitive Edge*. New York: John Wiley & Sons, 1984.

Hersh, Seymour M. *The Price of Power*. New York: Simon and Schuster, 1983.

Hicks, Jonathan P. "The Takeover of American Industry." *The New York Times*, May 28, 1989, F1, F8.

Hoffman, W. Michael, and Moore, Jennifer M. *Business Ethics: Readings, and Cases in Corporate Morality*. New York: McGraw-Hill, 1984.

Holusha, John. "Beating Japan at Its Own Game." *The New York Times*, July 6, 1989, pp. F1, F8.

Hormats, Robert D. "West Economics and Security." *The New York Times*, January 18, 1985, p. A21.

Independent Commission on Disarmament and Security Issues. *Common Security: A Blueprint for Survival*. New York: Simon and Schuster, 1982.

Jonas, Norman. "The Hollow Corporation." *Business Week*, March 3, 1986, p. 58.

Klare, Michael. "The Arms Trade: Changing Patterns in the 1980's." *Third World Quarterly*, October 1987, pp. 1257–81.

———"Deadly Convergence: The Perils of the Arms Trade." *World Policy Journal* (Winter 1988–89): 142–68.

Lawrence, Paul R., and Dyer, Davis. *Renewing American Industry.* New York: The Free Press, 1985.

Leontieff, Wassily, and Duchin, Faye. *Military Spending: Facts and Figures, Worldwide Implications and Future Outlook.* New York: Oxford University Press, 1983.

Lewis, Paul. "World War II is Over, But the Standardization Battle Has Just Begun." *National Journal*, September 4, 1976, pp. 1248–54.

Littleton, A. C. *Accounting Evolution to 1900.* New York: American Institute Publishing Co., 1933.

McConnell, C. R. "Why is Productivity Slowing Down?" *Harvard Business Review* (March–April 1979) pp. 36-61.

McCoy, Charles S. *Management of Values.* Boston: Pitman, 1985.

McGarrah, Robert E. "An Arms Run Economy: Remembering Eisenhower's Warning." *Christian Science Monitor*, November 20, 1984, pp. 29–30.

———. "A Better Strategy for Soviet Containment." *Christian Science Monitor*, July 15, 1981, p. 23.

———. "The Decline of U.S. Manufacturers: Causes and Remedies." *Business Horizons*, Indiana University (November-December 1987): 59–67.

———. "Do Computerized Intelligence Systems Cause Artificial Management?" *Challenge Magazine of Economic Affairs* (November-December 1985): 38–43.

———. "Expanding the Role of Higher Education, Regional Economic Development." In *Business and Academia: Partners in New England's Economic Revival*, edited by J. C. Hoy and M. Bernstein. Boston: University Press of New England, 1982.

———. "The Impact of Arms Exports to Nonaligned Nations." *East-West Outlook.* Washington, D.C.: American Committee on U.S.-Soviet Relations. September 1986, pp. 2, 3.

———. "Let's Internationalize Defense Marketing." *Harvard Business Review* (May-June 1969): 146–55.

———. "Logistics for the International Manufacturer." *Harvard Business Review* (March-April 1966): 154–59.

———. "The Manager Must Break His Chains." *Business & Society Review* (First Quarter 1975): 41–42.

178   Selected Bibliography

―――. "Military Deterrence and Western Security." *Christian Science Monitor*, September 24, 1985, p. 16.

―――. "Restoring the University." *Educational Record*. Washington D.C.: American Council on Education, Summer 1980, pp. 50–56.

―――. *Study of the NATO Hawk Program*. Washington D.C.: Logistics Management Institute, 1965.

―――. "Swords Into Plowshares." *Harvard Business Review* (July-August 1970): 36–45.

―――. "U.S. Military-Industrial Complex, Cooperation Better Than Competition." *Christian Science Monitor*, January 13, 1988, p. 13.

―――. "U.S. Strategies for Industrial Growth and Western Security." *Parameters*, U.S. Army War College (December 1982): 62–70.

McGarrah, Robert E. with A. Elkins. "The Urban Industrial Complex." *Industry*, Associated Industries of Massachusetts, May 1970, pp. 49–52.

MacNeil, William. "Make Mine Myth." *The New York Times*, December 28, 1981.

Mark, Jerome. "Productivity and Costs in the Private Economy, 1974." *Monthly Labor Review*, U.S. Department of Labor, 1975, pp. 3–8.

Markham, James M. "For Europe a New Look: Bush Fixes U.S. Role As A Modest One." *The New York Times*, July 20, 1989, p. A9.

Meadows, D. and A. *Limits to Growth*. New York: Universe Books, 1972.

Melman, Seymour. *Pentagon Capitalism: The Political Enemy of War*. New York: McGraw-Hill, 1970.

―――. *The Permanent War Economy: American Capitalism in Decline*. New York: Simon & Schuster, 1974.

Miles, Gregory L. "Forging the New Bethlehem Steel Co." *Business Week*, June 6, 1989, pp. 106–108.

Mitchell, D. F. "Some Firms Resume Manufacturing in the U.S. After Foreign Fiascoes." *The Wall Street Journal*, October 4, 1986.

M.I.T. Commission on Industrial Productivity. *Made in America*. Cambridge, MA: M.I.T. Press, 1989.

Nader, Ralph. *Unsafe At Any Speed*. New York: Grossman, 1965.

Norman, James R. "Days of Rage at Yale B-School." *Business Week*, December 2, 1988, p. 36.

Ohmae, Kemchi. "Don't Blame It on Tokyo." *New Perspectives Quarterly* (Fall 1987): 36.

Owen, Henry, and Schultze, Charles. ed. *Setting National Priorities*. Washington D.C.: The Brookings Institution, 1978.

Porat, Marc Uri. *The Information Economy*. 9 Volumes. Washington, D.C.: U.S. Department of Commerce, 1977.

Rand Corporation. *Aircraft Co-Production and Procurement Strategy*. Report R. 450–PR. Santa Monica, CA, May 1967.

Reich, Robert B. *The Next Industrial Frontier*. New York: Penguin Books, 1983.

Ryan, J. K., and Mitchell, L. "The Changing Fears of American Foreign Trade." *Business Marketing*, January 1981, pp. 49–57.

Sanderson, S. W. "American Industry Can Go Home Again." *Across the Board* (February 1986): 38.

Sanger, David E. "Mighty MITI Looses Its Grip." *The New York Times*, July 9, 1989, pp. F1, F9.

Schaffer, Robert H. "Motivating Workers: How To Tap the 'Zest Factor.' " *The New York Times*, May 7, 1989, p. F3.

Schellhardt, Timothy D., and Hymoulitz, Carol. "U.S. Manufacturers Face Changes in Years Ahead." *The Wall Street Journal*, May 2, 1989, sec. A, p. 2.

Scherer, Ron. "U.S. Debates Policy on Europe in 1992." *Christian Science Monitor*, May 18, 1989, p. 1.

Schneidar, Keith. "Big Farm Companies Try Hand at Organic Methods." *The New York Times*, May 28, 1989, pp. 1, 24.

Sethi, S. Prakash. "Corporations, United States Foreign Policy and Ethics of Overseas Operations: The ITT Affair." *Up Against the Corporate Wall*. 2d ed. Englewood Cliffs, NJ: Prentice Hall, 1974.

Shabecoff, Phillip. "The Environment: It's Time to Stop Treating Pollution and Depletion of Resources as Economic Assets." *The New York Times*, June 29, 1989, p. 37.

Stone, Peter. "Boom Days for Political Risk Consultants." *The New York Times*, August 7, 1983, pp. F1, F23.

Taylor, Lance. "The Costly Arms Trade." *The New York Times*, December 22, 1981, p. A19.

Thompson, D. B. "Exodus: Where is U.S. Industry Going?" *Industry Week*, January 6, 1986, p. 28.

Uchitelle, Louis. "Trade Business and Dollar Savings Raise Appeal of Factories Abroad: American Companies Turn Away From Exports." *The New York Times*, March 26, 1989, pp. F1, F23.

———. "U.S. Businesses Loosen Link to Mother Country." *The New York Times*, May 31, 1989, pp. D1, D30.

United Nations. *Economic and Social Consequences of the Arms Race and of Military Expenditures*. Report of the Secretary General, New York, 1978.

U.S. Arms Control and Disarmament Agency. *World Military Expenditures and Arms Transfers*. Washington, D.C.: U.S. Government Printing Office, 1986, 1987.

U.S. Bureau of Labor Statistics. *Structure of the U.S. Economy, 1980 and 1985*. Washington, D.C.: U.S. Government Printing Office, 1975.

U.S. General Accounting Office. *Foreign Military Sales, A Potential Drain on the U.S. Defense Posture*. September 2, 1977.

————. *Improvements Still Needed in Recouping Costs of Foreign Military Sales*. Washington, D.C., February 2, 1982.

————. *Military Sales to Iran*, 1974.

U.S. State Department. *U.S.-European Cooperation in Military Technology*. Arlington, VA.: Ex-Im Tech, Inc., 1974.

Wantuck, Kenneth A., "The ABC's of Japanese Productivity." *Production and Inventory Management Review* (September 1981): 22–28.

Wilber, Charles K, ed. *The Political Economy of Development and Underdevelopment*. New York: Random House, 1979.

Willens, Harold. *The Trimtab Factor*. New York: William Morrow, 1984.

White, Joseph B. "Auto Mechanics Struggle to Cope with Technology in Today's Cars." *Wall Street Journal*, July 26, 1988, p. 37.

Yarmolinsky, Adam. *The Military Establishment*. New York: Harper and Row, 1971.

Index

About the Author

ROBERT E. MCGARRAH is Professor of Management at the University of Massachusetts, Amherst. He served as Assistant Director, International Research & Engineering Programs, Office of the Secretary of Defense; Vice President, Logistics Management Institute for U.S. defense procurement policies; Assistant Director, International Division, U.S. General Accounting Office; and as consultant on production-operations management for major U.S. manufacturing companies, as well as the author of numerous books and journal articles on the U.S. government's and manufacturers' policies affecting productivity, corporate morale and market competitiveness.